The Lost Guru

Uncover The Mental Habits That Prevent You From Fully Inhabiting Your Life And Accessing Your Intrinsic Wisdom

By Amethyst and Greg Dickson

ISBN: 978-1-7770774-1-9

Dedication

This is our first book together as co-founders and co-conspirators in the dream that is the Life Origami Corporation. This Book is dedicated to our kids, friends and family that have been on this journey with us. Thanks to everyone for the emotional support we have received. We truly are dancing in our dreams awake.

"To Amethyst, my wife, you make my heart sing. This journey began when we began to believe in love again, learning to love ourselves first. We went our separate ways and then much later, opened our hearts to the Universe. Then when we reunited 10 years later, fireworks erupted in my heart — we married — now everyday is like a grande adventure. I am grateful that we have this opportunity to not only reunite and live out the rest of our lives together — we are choosing to explore writing this book and operating this business together. The world is a better place because we have come together. I am grateful to be able to live and work with my soul mate!"

> *"I can't change the wind or the sea... I can adjust my sails and tack towards my destination." Amethyst Dickson*

"To Greg, heart of my heart, you are the epitome of my favourite cherished soul to be sharing this journey with, this adventure we call OUR life. I feel we truly are "Loving Life and Learning Together".

Introduction

Who this book is for and what you can expect

You have worked hard all your life. You have jumped through the hoops. You have **dedicated yourself** to looking after your family and/or a business. Despite all your hard work and good intentions, you still find yourself **wondering what's next for you**. Life's responsibilities abound, there were and always will be changing economic conditions, societal pressures, duties, and practical realities you have to deal with. That is just a fact of life. It is these realities which have actually shaped you. They have **brought you to this moment in time**, reading this book.

We believe you have decided that **this is your time**. This is an opportunity for you to **invest** some focused time, effort and **energy on yourself**. You are **ready to take a deeper look** at the life you have created and explore what **might be possible**. You are ready to begin exploring what **types of changes** you could make. You know there are aspects of your life which must change. We applaud you, this is a great place to be! This represents an **opportunity to give yourself a break** and embrace what could become your second act, and to decide "What's it going to be". Its time to **take a closer look** and ask yourself "who has been writing my life's script, and how do I begin to change it?"

> You realize in order to keep pace with a continuously changing and evolving world, **you are going to have to change** and evolve too.

Despite your best efforts to serve others and "fit in", you find yourself doubting your ability to **step into the fullness** of what you could become. You feel an underlying tension to fill an unidentified gap and hole within. You have done your best to do everything others said you "should do". You have bought and read the books, attended the webinars/seminars/workshops, and somehow, still **feel there is something missing**. You know there are areas of your life where you are not living up to your potential.

You feel like there is **something more out there for you**, but it seems vague and overwhelming.

On the other hand, maybe you are the person who just wants the data, the facts. You think that the source of your problems is not having the **right** information. You may think, "After all, if I get the **right information** then I will be able to figure out what the **logical next step** should be".

Maybe, you are simply the kind of person who **just wants the results** "damn it". You think that your biggest problem is that you just need to get into action. You want to bypass all the emotional cruft, not waste time, and **get moving**.

Perhaps you are the person who takes **pride** in being the most friendly, open person you know. You **always show up** for your friends and family. You tend to be obsessed with filling your calendar and keeping busy. You are so busy being a professional, a real friend and supporting your family, that you **have little real time for yourself**. Often you wonder, "Why can't we all just get along?" Or you may think, "I'll find time for myself next week." Next week comes and goes, and you still **struggle to put your needs first**.

It's possible, right now, that **life is great** and you feel like you are living the dream. Yet, deep down there is a **secret** anxiety that you never let anybody see or talk about. You find it **hard to rest and relax** because you want to **make the most** of this part of your life. You have more money and think you are more successful and have a better quality life than most of the people you know. Yet, you wonder, by your own standards, "will I ever truly arrive or be able to rest and relax?"

Whether you identify with one or all of the above perspectives that people tend to have, there are at least **ten characteristics**, common amongst **people who are fully inhabiting their life**. These include:

1. **Face The Truth About Change**: They understand that without conscious awareness, focus and true intent to change there will be no difference.
2. **Self Knowledge IS The Beginning Of Mastery**: They make a decision to stop listening to others, and begin to tap into their own self knowledge archive, and explore self-mastery.
3. **The Ability To See Things As They Are**: The magic of living a fully inhabited life is the ability to see life, people and circumstances as they are. To see "things the way they actually are" i.e. reality. They don't get all wrapped up in wishing things were different.
4. **Develop A Conscious, Intentional Mindset**: The one thing that affects everything else in their life, is their mindset, which is congruent with their values and beliefs. This is the definition of integrity. When they live according to their own standards, then they realize that they are being true to themselves.
5. **Know The Difference Between Goals Versus Results**: They don't set goals if they aren't clear about what they want, or have a compelling vision. They do not waste time chasing after vague ideas, without a specific, meaningful and defined result or outcome.
6. **Step Out Of The Comfort Zone**: For real change to occur, they know they must continually be learning, and integrating it. They understand that change only occurs outside their comfort zone. They know doing the same old thing will result in the same old results.
7. **Confront Their Resistance To Change**: They are always willing to pay attention to any resistance and tension, because they know it will interfere with change. They are willing to embrace self accountability, responsibility, and lean-in to the opportunity to try something new.
8. **Constantly Acquiring & Developing New Skills**: They are students of life. They have the ability to extract valuable lessons, insights and key distinctions from any experience, positive or negative.
9. **Practice, Practice, Practice**: They know that there are times when nothing replaces practice and they actively seek training opportunities - to increase their self-awareness and competence.

10. **Open And Ready To Grow**: They are coachable and realize that there are times when they just need to "think out loud" with a trusted, experienced confidante.

The question is, where do you go now, in order to learn these ten fundamental characteristics?

Many people look to an outside source like a Guru who seems to have all the answers in life. Yet, by doing this, we miss out on the greatest opportunity to know who we are and what we want. Now you may be wondering where a person can turn to find the answers. Here is a thought to consider:

> What if there was a Guru who had a **treasure trove of wisdom and insights** customized for you? You would want to meet that Guru, right?

The truth is **that Guru**, who has been storing up all those insights, distinctions and wisdom for you — **is within you**.

> That's right, **you are** The Lost Guru™.

If this is true then why have you not heard of this before?

The reason is you have been separated from your Lost Guru. Your inner voice has been drowned out by the projections, judgments and negative dialogue of the ego. This occurs because the ego's anxious and paranoid voice dominates your quiet, subtle inner voice. The reason this is so important is your inner voice speaks from the context of your entire lifetime. So exposing the ego is imperative to being able to connect with your inner voice. You are faced with a choice. You can choose to continue to dance with the ego, other people's agendas, or instead follow the lead of your lost guru. Dances with the active witness and the ego are very different. There is a different rhythm, tone and energy of the arrogant ego versus the quiet, subtle inner voice of your lost guru.

It's like they are singing different lyrics to your favourite song, that is your life. The ego tends to be insecure, angry and fearful. The inner voice is quiet, unassuming, gentle and supportive. The inner voice is never critical, judgemental or unkind. It simply reflects the reality and truth from your life experience, all with an eye to what is in your best interest. The inner voice awaits your inquiry and interest, whereas the ego busts in and disrupts your party. It enjoys another type of party - the infamous pity party. Its a party theme with different guests who are there to flog you with their opinions and conditioning.

We have been **conditioned** to automatically trust the people who seem to know what they are doing. We have been taught to look up to them, follow and mimic them. Some other gurus even recommend that you model yourself after them. They suggest that choosing to model yourself after someone else will shorten your learning curve. How so? The assumption is that if you follow their methods — which they created and learned from the context of their own lives — you'll bypass your learning curve. Except, they aren't you and you aren't them.

When you follow their life lessons, you miss out on the opportunity to extract the insights and lessons from your own life. In our experience, if anything, following others how-to manuals — tends to lengthen your learning curve. It actually wastes the time, effort, energy and resources spent trying to fit the square peg of their life into the context (aka round hole) of your life experience. You loose twice, you waste the time spent trying to assimilate their methods and you also lost the opportunity to spend that time on **something you do and know already**.

You actually have heard of "The Lost Guru™", you just **know it by a number of different labels** and descriptors. Perhaps you have heard people talk about their intuition, that still small voice, little heart, sixth sense, gut feeling, clairvoyance, second sight and instinct. Whatever label you prefer matters not, it does not change the fact that it exists.

> The question and the challenge is, how do you access your lifetime of wisdom and insights? The short answer is that you have to **build a relationship** with "The Lost Guru™" within.

Take heart, from a Life Origami™ perspective every human was born with an **"active witness™", a fellow traveller.** This active witness, The Lost Guru™, has seen everything you've ever done, heard every word you've ever spoken or has been spoken to you. It also has **observed everything that has happened to you**, it never shuts off. It has the **full context** of your entire life experience. We have not been taught how to tap into the richness of our life experiences. In fact, we have forgotten that we were once living in harmony with our active witness. As we have matured we gradually learned to replace it with others knowledge and intelligence. All of this is the result of our tendency toward over-analyzing, over-thinking everything.

In fact, you most likely edit, modify and limit your potential to being able to tap into your greatness. When you do this, you are **denying your own capabilities, intelligence and experiences**. This is often the result of having too much respect for fear, failure and success. So you may replace your inner voice as the ego gets caught up trying to avoid failure, and then you don't allow yourself to **explore your full capabilities**. When this occurs you are not fully engaged and do not embrace your greatness.

The Lost Guru™, your "active witness" is like a documentary film crew that has been **following you** throughout your entire life. It has been recording everything from the moment you were born. You can **learn to access** the information, from The Lost Guru™. To do this, you have to learn how to **connect** with your active witness (a.k.a. The Lost Guru) When you make that connection, you will gain access to your **lifetime of accumulated wisdom**.

As children and young adults, we **gradually disconnect** from the active witness, as we retreat into our "thinking-ness". This thinking-ness has become second nature and has been reinforced throughout our lives. It is the combination of parental, societal, educational and work place expectations.

We have a lifetime of experiences, thoughts, beliefs, morals, ethics and values, from others, that we have adopted and assimilated. Some of them serve us, and **many of them inhibit our ability to live life on our own terms.** We have to learn how to sort and sift through them all, in order to identify the ones which **serve our highest good** and which do not. Until we do that, we will struggle to tap into The Lost Guru™'s treasure of lifelong wisdom.

The first step in finding The Lost Guru™ is to **uncover the mental habits which are preventing you from being able to access the guru within**. This is the beginning of uncovering the roadblocks, which are preventing you from tapping into the wisdom of your life. That is what this book is about.

The truth is, if you truly want to experience a sense of clarity, liberty and freedom — **now is the time** to examine your mental habits.

> **Until you get to know** what you think and whether it is still relevant to your life today, you will be vulnerable to the worlds priorities and other people's agendas.

Everybody we have worked with, including successful achievers - on some level they all struggled to cope with uncertainty. They grappled with a **nagging feeling**, that in someway, they were "**not enough**".

Why is this? We all fall under the umbrella of other people's concepts, beliefs and values. These become seemingly invisible rules which operate in our **subconscious minds, and influence how we think**, act and make decisions. This impacts what we believe is possible for us and how we feel about ourselves.

It is a **natural** human characteristic to be influenced by others. Everywhere we go in life, family, friends, everything in the media and online tells us what to do, how to think, and attempt to get us to adopt what they think is ethical or moral. All of us have people who tell us what they think constitutes a successful life, according to their own will, whims and wishes. This can create a feeling that we are not enough. Yet, their version of how they define success, **may not be anything close to what you desire**.

They project their opinions, beliefs, dogma and patterns onto you. At first blush, these perspectives might seem reasonable, however, they may not be valid for you. **You are an individual with unique life experiences.** You have gone through many defining moments and they have made you who you are today. Every single conversation you have ever had, accompanied by all the feelings and thoughts that are associated with them, accumulate to make you who you are. So what someone else tells you to do or think, and how to do it, may not be relevant. It may not serve your higher good.

> What is important is that you **stay curious** enough to **enter your learning curve**, and discover **who you are** and how you learn.

You do not need to run after any other guru's opinions and understandings. It is after all, based on the context of their life, not yours. **What counts is what you think.** How you got to where you are today has to do with **the way you think**. The way you think is a result of the stories and patterns that have proven to be effective for you throughout your life.

We all learn and grow through defining moments in life, and then graduate onto the next moment. The **wisdom of your life is cumulative** as you successfully move through it, examining the feedback from your actions and decisions, and **learning** from it.

If someone else tells you what to do, think or feel, and you don't examine it - it probably isn't going to help you in the long run. It **could become a roadblock** to fully getting to know yourself and honouring your journey. You need to learn how you learn according to "**You-How**, not They-How".

> This inner wisdom is available for you to tap into, and **create movement** in your life. If this is so, why have you not been able to live fully and get the movement you need? Why does anxiety still plague you?

What you need to **learn is how to evaluate your thoughts** and determine whether or not they are helping you move forward. If not, you could end up taking yourself out of the game and not even realize it.

You might think you know yourself, and are well on your way to get what you want. Yet, you may still be experiencing anxiety, worry, grieving, negative self talk and story telling of past childhood woes. This is a type of **disguised, invisible fear** that may actually be holding you captive and preventing you from getting what you want. You may feel like you don't know what you want.

> You deserve to **live your life according to your own standards** of what brings you joy, significance and meaning.

When you follow other gurus, many of them will attempt to teach you their philosophy of change. Some people end up so steeped in the philosophers philosophies, that they cannot see why they aren't getting what they want in life. They are **caught running on the treadmill** of trying to digest and assimilate these obscure philosophies.

These know-it-all Gurus, often don't show you how to get in touch with the wisdom of **your** life experience. You may have all their worksheets, swipe files, templates, read their books, attended their events/workshops. Yet, you still struggle to feel at peace, calm and relaxed.

We think **you deserve something that is long lasting and sustainable**; this can only come from having a relationship with your lost guru. When you learn to tap into your inherent strengths, skills, wisdom and abilities of The Lost Guru™, this will set you up to **take on any challenge** in life.

Reading this book is the beginning of helping yourself to **become familiar with the active witness** of your life (aka The Lost Guru™).

> To do that you need to learn how to hear The Lost Guru's voice. Which means you need to learn to **distinguish between your voice and the noise of the world** and your own paranoid, anxious and fearful thought patterns. **That is what this book is all about**.

Our goal is to help you understand how to **navigate the ocean of your own thoughts**, first. Otherwise your own voice and thoughts will drown out the still, subtle, gentle voice of The Lost Guru™.

If the ideas you have been reading resonate with you, you will enjoy the rest of the book and continue your journey of self-discovery.

You can make progress by becoming aware of what is working for you and what is not. You can figure out who you are and who you aren't, what you want more of or less of. **New skills and tools** will be required to get you from where you are today, to where you deserve to be.

Your first step is to begin to **explore the possibility** that you have an inner, lost guru. And of course, the only way to access the guru within, is to figure out the **mental habits which have been preventing** you from accessing the wisdom of your life. This is the beginning of your quest to meet The Lost Guru™.

At Life Origami we serve people from a wide range of religions, beliefs and philosophies. We make no distinction or judgment about what you believe. We are simply presenting an observation about the human condition and the active witness that has been travelling with you throughout your entire life. In our experience, this awareness of the active witness is solid, dependable, and once uncovered — transformational. There's nothing you can do to turn the active witness off, its always on. However, you can learn to tap into its wisdom. At Life Origami, we believe with practice you can cultivate a relationship with your active witness as a resource to guide you.

Read on because **the answers you seek are within you** and will be revealed as you **reflect upon what you are reading**. You will slowly peel away the layers of other people's agendas, beliefs and rules. You will, with each page, get to know what's been holding you back from looking deeper within.

Reading this book is your first step on your Guru path.

You will observe four core messages woven throughout this book:

1. The **Guru** you seek is **already** within you.
2. You don't know what you want, **even though you think you do**. This is because you haven't spent the time to discover your deeper desires. You stop yourself because on some level, in some areas of your life you feel you aren't enough. You feel you aren't worthy of more, so you don't indulge the idea. You don't **trust yourself with the dream** in the first place.
3. We all commit the **Ultimate Crime, we deny our weaknesses and our greatness**. We do this because we are not confronting and examining the roadblocks to our success.
4. **Growing and learning together** is most important as you navigate the path of communication and connection **in relationships** on the road toward fully inhabiting your life.

There is one thing we know for sure. You **do not have to** live any longer with doubt, anxiety, confusion, frustration or self loathing. Your Lost Guru™ has been collecting your memories, experiences and life context, keeping them safe for you. We are here to tell you that **you can learn how to unlock your mind and your heart to access your greatness**. This book will awaken you to the obstacles, habits and patterns which have **kept The Lost Guru™ just out of your reach.**

We are going to stop here and resist the urge to explain and summarize this entire book. **The trick is to read it, contemplate it and see if there is a part of you that awakens while reading it.** We extend an invitation to dialogue with us about your journey, on Facebook in our Life Origami group.

1. You Can Tap Into The Inherent Wisdom Of Your Lost Guru

You Have An Active Witness To Your Life, Meet Your Lost Guru

What if YOU are The Lost Guru™?

> That's right! Believe it or not, we think that **you** are your own best teacher, guide and guru.

You have access and can tap into the wisdom that **you have accumulated** over your lifetime. You are also the **only one who can tap into the context** of this inner guru and use it to **guide yourself** through life.

Some of us believe we don't have enough knowledge, skills or abilities to meet life's challenges on our own. Perhaps you have felt this way at times.

> We want you to know that **you don't need anyone to fix you**, because ***you are NOT broken***.

By making a simple adjustment to learn, "how you learn" you can reconnect with your Lost Guru™. We like to think of it as the **"active witness"** to your entire life. Through learning to access your active witness, your ability to adapt and learn will quickly accelerate.

Even though at times in your life you might have felt lost, anxious, confused or frustrated — **you have never been lost**. At times, you may have felt **disoriented and bewildered** by the rapid pace of change. Perhaps you have even felt baffled and humbled by life. This can happen to anyone, at anytime, and is a normal reaction when we hit speed bumps in life. What is not normal is staying stuck, feeling beaten, broken, confused or battered.

> *We have good news. When you were born your "active witness" began recording everything. Learning to access its context is the key that opens the* ***treasure chest that is your life experience***.

Think about that. If that is true, you owe it to yourself to keep reading.

> *There is a part of you which came into* ***conscious*** *realization, from the moment you were conceived. This presence* ***has always been an "active witness"*** *to the experiences in your life. It has been present* ***from the moment you were conceived***.

While in the womb taking form, your consciousness was simply being present with the physical. Your non-physical consciousness was harmonizing with your growing mortal, developing physical presence.

At the moment of birth, you were immediately thrust into your physical plane of existence. While the birthing experience felt physically traumatic, your conscious presence **also experienced a "sense separation"**. Your body experienced the physical separation from your mother. However, despite this feeling of separation, we do not believe that you were ever separated from your non-physical "presence" (i.e. consciousness).

Since the moment of your birth, you have been on a continuous quest of sorting, exploring, reconciling and seeking to make sense of this separation experience. What you need to understand is this experience of birth **feels like separation, but only on the physical level**.

At the level of non-physical (consciousness), **no separation ever actually occurred** and never will. Even when your physical body is no longer animate, the non-physical presence, your consciousness is undisturbed. We believe it existed before you were conceived and will continue forward after your animate tether disconnects in the physical plane called your body.

When you are born, an animation begins and you become lively and engaged. Literally, what happens at conception is cells divide and your body takes shape (heart and mind). And then poof, you are born! You are thrust into reality from the womb. Then - we go Waaaaaaaah! LOL

It is possible to resolve this "sense of separation" and gain a powerful, congruent experience of life. It will assist you in moving forward, confidently and congruently in the present, in the here and now. You **can** reconnect with your "active witness". We **invite** you to **think of it** as **your "Lost Guru", rediscovered.**

> *As you get reacquainted, you will experience a rapid connection with the fullness and wisdom of your life.*

Gradually you will become **familiar and explore a relationship with your "Lost Guru",** you will begin to experience a **new frame of reference**. What was once confusing or obscure, will very quickly morph into a very tangible **birds-eye-view of your life**. Past problems, puzzles and the mysteries that disturbed and befuddled you, are now of little importance. Where once doubt, fear and anxiety ruled the day, a new tangible sense of self-hood becomes accessible.

As you embrace this new awareness, **you will begin to perceive** your life in a more complete context. This fullness of seeing yourself, will transmute the obscure, vague and opaque aspects of your life, into striking clarity. Those aspects will be resolved so you can get on with "fully inhabiting" your life.

> *This will present you with numerous opportunities to tap into the power of non-physical, conscious insights, inspiration and perspectives.*

Describing Your Active Witness (a.k.a. Lost Guru)

The active witness knows how you feel about certain things. This occurs because it has been actively present, observing every aspect of your life. Even as you naturally attempt to control your life or deal with the influence of other people's points of view. The active witness knows how you feel about certain things even though you might feel confused.

For the most part, you have been **absorbing the opinions, beliefs and values of others,** your entire life. These adopted views and beliefs become embedded in your subconscious. They may or may not be beneficial to you. Your Active Witness is the ***antidote*** *to the programmed, subconscious automatic reactions* which have been accumulating and shaping your life.

You know these influences from others, have been coming at you all throughout your life. Other people will always exert a certain amount of influence over us. You can gain control over these influences by learning how to tap into the wisdom of your active witness. As a result, you can escape repeating the painful experiences of the past.

When you are under the subconscious influence of others you end up chasing other people's ideals, dreams and rainbows. So this active witness knows deep down who you are and what you really want.

To get closer to this reality you will need to understand what stops you from connecting with this active witness, your Lost Guru. What stops you is that you don't know what you really want.

You Don't Know What You Want (You "Think" You Do, That's A BIG Problem)

> *We know you **think** you actually **do know** what you want i.e. less **stress,** increased **happiness, personal growth** or perhaps more **success**. These are not "goals" they are **broad generalizations** and chasing them **destroys your drive and impedes making real movement towards what you really want to experience**.*

Keep reading and you will learn why this idea, that you "think you know what you want" could be a bigger obstacle than you might imagine.

> *You just might gain an insight or two when you understand why **the belief** that you "think you know what you want" might actually be your **Achilles heel. It very well could be what is preventing you from experiencing what makes your heart sing**.*

Even though you think you are experiencing less stress, enjoying increased revenue or have a better job, are feeling productive — you might still be feeling like there is more for you. Why? Your **goals might be so broad** (like the examples above) and lacking in specifics that it is difficult to identify when you've achieved it. If you cannot easily quantify what your results are i.e. being successful, you will not be able to adjust and adapt to create it.

These broad generalizations lull you into a comfortable complacency. This happens because **when your goals are so generic** you do not feel regret, any sense of accomplishment or the creative tension which naturally arises from a **need for completion**.

> *When your goals are lacking specificity, it is* ***too easy for you to let yourself off the hook****.*

Unfortunately, when you let yourself off the hook, you also do not experience any sense of fulfillment or achievement. As you are reading this, right now, you might be experiencing cognitive dissonance — a general unease and mental discomfort with what you are reading.

It's okay. This is normal.

When you are presented with new evidence that seems to contradict your beliefs, values or ideas of how "things are supposed to work" — this clash can make you **feel uncomfortable. This is good.** Your comfort zone is really a trap. Remember, real **change *always* lies outside** your comfort zone.

> *Perhaps you cope by numbing out with video games or keeping yourself busy with friends, meetings, activities, social media or other "projects". This is* ***because*** *they feel familiar and comfortable.*

You might justify your behaviours saying to yourself, "I deserve a little me time to myself. After all, I've been busy." This rationalizes your over indulgence and obsessive need to keep busy and avoid reality.

Know this, it is not your fault.

Before you ditch this concept and move onto something more "constructive" — stick around — at least until we show you what could be preventing you from **creating movement in your life or business**.

The uncomfortable truth is, if you had clarity around what you want, you wouldn't feel an ***awkward tension, discontent*** *or low level of unease.*

We believe you are a person with a strong work ethic, integrity and clear sense of morality. There is no doubt that you've dedicated yourself to your profession and/or helping family members, employees or others in your community. You are proud and rightly so, of the contribution you are making.

You might be thinking that this book is not for you. After all, things aren't that bad and are actually pretty good. It would be natural to assume that there is no reason to believe you couldn't just continue doing things the way you always have. Yet, there is "one little thing" eating away at you...

On some level, you **know there is more for you**, *much more to life than what you are currently experiencing.*

In fact, deep down inside of you, there is an awareness that you have **capabilities, opportunities and untapped potential** that you've not fully experienced.

Right now there could be a little voice eating away at your identity and self-confidence. On some level you feel like a bit of a pretender, an imposter. On some level you feel like you are "not enough". And even more chilling — by your own standards — you secretly wonder if you'll ever be able to fully experience what **you know** you are **capable of truly achieving**.

We think this little voice (a.k.a fear of failure or missing out) has been needling you long enough. It has been chirping away and subtly sowing seeds of doubt. Or perhaps the nastiest one of them all, "You're not focused and productive enough. **You can do better.**"

Therefore, you tried to control what you could and got into action and ignored the rest. But now you've hit a wall. Your effectiveness is

> ***not what it used to be**. You feel confused and stressed more than you'd like. Yet, you keep pushing ahead. Despite your best efforts, you **feel empty and keep yourself busy**, hoping you'll stumble onto something that might be the magic pill.*

There is no **magic** pill.

You might **want the quick fix**, however the quick fix rarely resolves ingrained habitual patterns and persistent problems. Here is the thing, you still have to **choose what you want to experience** "more" of or "less" of in your life.

> *Until you get **crystal clear about what you want** — you are, most likely, wasting some of the most significant moments of your life.*

When this happens, your life ends up being consumed within the no-mans-land of doubt, ambiguity and procrastination. No one wants that, and yet when that happens, you could end up **chasing the wrong thing, at the wrong time for the wrong reason**. Not only that, you end up wasting the time that could've been spent actually resolving the issue.

> *Days turn into months, months into years — years you can never get back, unless you learn how to **redeem those lost opportunities.***

You can redeem lost opportunities and open the door to new opportunities. All you need to do is to take the time to get clear about ***what*** you want.

> *We have been telling our clients for decades, "You **can** get anything you want. **First** you need to know "**what"** you want."*

Manifesting and living your dreams isn't really that difficult, however, **you will have to choose**. Surprisingly, choosing is one of the most difficult things, especially when we are confused, tired or frustrated.

*The good news? Once you know what you want, it gets a **lot easier**.*

From that point forward, it is just a matter of learning how to **invest your time, effort, energy** and **resources** into your wants and desires.

*Truly, anything is possible, but **first** you must choose what you want.*

Sounds easy right? Before you can get started you will first need to rid yourself of a nasty thinking virus called "productivity and performance hacking". Why? These so called "productivity and performance hacks" could be the silent killer of your dreams. The reason productivity and performance hacking is so attractive is **we crave and thirst for the easy answers.** This drive for easy answers is also part of the problem. Keep reading, you're closer to an important insight than you might imagine.

There Is No Hack To Bypassing Your Learning Curve

*Your recurring life or business challenges cannot be resolved through improving performance or tweaking productivity alone. **You have to get to the root of rotten thinking.** As it is surreptitiously draining your strength, sense of purpose and killing your momentum.*

Have you ever thought "I just wish I could stop taking myself out of the game."

Do you find yourself setting goals and then dropping them, or never starting them in the first place?

The problem isn't procrastination, accountability or motivation — there is nothing wrong with you, you have been **infected with a thought virus.**

What is this thought virus?

It's thinking that if you can incrementally improve your productivity you will get more work done in the same or less amount of time.

While at first blush, this idea of getting more done in the same, or less amount of time is appealing, it does not address the bigger issue.

*This bigger issue is that long-term accomplishment requires long-term performance, which is realized **only** when there is **long-term, consistent learning**. A long-term pattern of learning will also require unwavering, persistent attention to your thoughts and habits — over the long-term.*

Living In The Learning Curve IS Mastery

When we want to bring meaning to our lives, we **have to take a chance** on doing something different.

*We need to get out of our comfortable chairs and **enter the learning curve.***

There is **no skirting around or buying your way through the learning curve**. We have to learn and work our way through it. This work includes being willing and ready to **confront and examine** all the attitudes, fears and beliefs that might be holding us back. These fears are written into our subconscious with all the little stories that we have attached to and identified with. When we become attached to old stories and disappointments from the past, that we were worthless, or feel we are also in the present - those old stories will continue to surface in our future. When we do that we blow out the candlelight of being a "can-do person" who is on the path to mastery.

***Students of self-mastery follow their curiosity's** and fully inhabit their lives with ambition and passion.*

However, when we shrink back, this exhilaration and passion does not fully come to fruition in our life experiences. Regarding shrinking back: Remember, as long as we hold back from acknowledging our greatness and our knowledge/intellect, we are not embracing our capabilities and our full potential to learn.

Keep Going When The Learning Gets Tough (Mastering Momentum)

Noel Burch, an employee with Gordon Training International, used the Conscious Competence Ladder in the 1970s. The four stages of the ladder suggest that, we are initially, **unaware of how little we actually know**. We are, in a very real sense, unconscious of our incompetence.

The theory explains that as we recognize our incompetence, we are moved to consciously acquire the skill. Then naturally, we will wish to use and apply what we have learned. This theory suggests that when it is utilized without being consciously thought through — we have then acquired unconscious competence. In other words, **we have become so good at it, that we are not even aware that we are doing it, while doing it.**

The four stages are **Unconscious Incompetence** (don't know what we don't know), **Conscious Incompetence** (we know what we do not know), **Conscious Competence**, you know "how" to do something, but it requires concentration and finally **Unconscious Competence**, we have so much practice it has literally become second nature, and can easily be performed, sometimes while doing another task. We would suggest that when you **cross over to Unconscious Competence you are entering into Mastery.**

> *In our opinion, **Mastery is a lifestyle and a mindset**, a way of thinking about learning. It is a demonstrated willingness to continue to be a student, to treat every piece of feedback and interaction as an opportunity to learn and grow.*

Over the course of our lives, we have met a few people we considered true masters. One thing was common — they were all **students first.** Each of them were open to learning and seemed like they could learn anything from anyone, even a complete newbie.

They were humble, present always (the active observer) and **their curiosity knew no bounds**. It was like life was their classroom. Nothing was off limits and they were eager and interested in people, their craft — anything which would expand their point-of-view and horizons. They were not intimidated by criticism, negative feedback and in the face of an argument or disagreement they still stood their ground, staying open and curious. It was more important to them to always be **learning from the feedback** than to be right.

> *This bears repeating, they were students even at their advanced level. They always seemed to somehow maintain the humility and curiosity of a new student. More and most impressive, they were comfortable being themselves and yet always open to insights, distinctions and learning.*

These masters never became complacent or fell into the trap of the comfort zone because **they knew it would keep them from stepping into their power.** They would often laugh when discovering an insight, whoever and wherever the source. There was no pretence because they were always learning and teaching — often at the same time.

Living As A Perpetual Student

These masters were willing to try anything, talk about anything and when you asked a question that they had not heard before — they would stop, look you in the eye, chuckle and say something like "Is that so? Isn't that interesting." Or "Tell me more." Nothing was off limits and they respected everyone regardless of their experience, appearance or position of power.

In fact, the more impressed other people were with themselves and their perception of their abilities — the more agile the masters became in handling them. They could dispense with silly people like ants. Never becoming disturbed or pretentious, they would wryly mock these self important people with subtle humour.

The way they viewed life and people was simple. They seemed to observe people from one of three perspectives — rigid, flexible or silly. They adored and studied the flexible people, had pity and little time for the rigid and inflexible. They were remarkably nimble dispatching missives to the silly souls who might cross their paths. When people would attempt to assert their intellect, they still respected them because in the Masters world each person represents an opportunity for the Master to learn and grow.

Most important, they **never left the learning curve** and always did the work required to **achieve unconscious competence**. Truth is, their "work" felt more like play. Like a kid playing and mixing paint for the first time.

They were always **willing to explore** something new and could turn any task into a play date — which was their real "art". They played with their work and worked at their play. They seemed to effortlessly solve problems by embracing the art **and** science of their craft. The science lies in their ability to correlate cause and effect — while still ***in*** the learning curve. Their art is the creative exploration of their observations and their relentless pursuit of excellence and applying what they learned.

The Art of a Life Well Lived

Art, is a strange and wonderful thing, some might say even mystical. Yet, when you are in the presence of "art" you feel it. This is because the artist has revealed something that we identify with when viewing their art. For example, a sculptor, sees an image in the marble, even when it is a boring hunk of rock. Slowly the artist removes material to uncover the image that they see hidden within the stone.

This same opportunity is available to us in this life. If we learn to take the ***sculptors perspective*** *— the image of* ***what you want in your life is already present****.*

It is your job as the sculptor to reveal it by shedding the unnecessary material, baggage and bulk accumulated as we move through life. If you are disciplined, slowly, you will begin chipping away at the extra and unnecessary weight of life. This is the effortless unfolding of a life of ease.

When you ***allow*** *all life and nature to be what it needs to be, then you will be exploring your relationship with life, like it is an unfolding work of art. You will begin to feel your momentum start to build.*

Exploring The Art Of Building Momentum

The impetus of momentum (aka energy) gained by a moving object is like a flywheel. A flywheel is attached between the crank shaft and the ignition system which triggers the starter and begins to move the flywheel of the engine. The heaviness of the flywheel stores the potential, kinetic energy and smooths the operation of a reciprocating engine. The flywheel is heavy, the stored energy is captured by the weight of the flywheel and used to increase the engines momentum and smooth movement.

The potential energy captured in the large mass overcomes the resistance (inertia) to movement. The energy then becomes dynamic and movement is effortless; less force is required to maintain it. With all movement, energy is expended and motion occurs. It will eventually lose its momentum unless it has continuous energy added. But, it takes less energy to keep it going than initially, when there was greater inertia.

There is the example of when you can't seem to start a car and decide to push start it. Initially, the hardest part is getting it going. Once in motion, less force and effort is needed to keep it going. Momentum builds and the combined weight of the flywheel and cars momentum combine to maintain momentum.

The momentum of the flywheel helps us in our lives too. The **intention to learn and expand overcomes** your own **human inertia**. **When something is learned once, it can be applied again.**

> *In our program, we assert that Mastering the Art of Momentum occurs when your mindset, skills, tools, training and coaching add energy and power to the* ***flywheel of your learning curve — of your life****. You become a net positive energy generator and an energy resource, which over the course of time adds momentum to your life. Your actions become more refined, accurate and effortless.*

To live consistently in your learning curve, you will need to step into a heightened level of self-expression and tap into your drive to thrive.

The Drive To Thrive

We interact with our "drive to thrive" through the lens of self-expression, self-efficacy and self-care.

> *We believe, the drive to thrive — is as important as oxygen is to our very survival.*

Just like it takes two atoms to make oxygen, we think the "drive to thrive" is fuelled by embracing both self-expression and self-efficacy.

At Life Origami we view **Self-Expression** as the **Second Law of Individuality™**. Like gravity, self expression is always a force in everyone's life. Just like the law of gravity, we cannot see or hold self-expression, but we feel and experience the "effects" of it constantly.

*The Law of Self Expression (a.k.a. The Drive To Thrive™) is what occurs as we **embrace our essential being** and rise to **express** our thoughts, feelings and experiences.*

Earlier in our lives, it is an unconscious response; we just naturally explore our world and "play". As we grow older and have increased physical and mental capacity — we move into **conscious and intentional self-expression**.

*When we feel threatened or concerned about our self-efficacy (ability to effectively care for ourselves) we risk moving into **unconscious self-sabotage and survival.***

Essentially, there are five things everyone requires in order to survive, these include: air, food, water, shelter and sleep. The need to survive and to take action, in order to ensure our continued existence, is an unconscious vital urge that drives us forward.

Have you ever struggled to breathe? Within a moment, you know something is critically wrong. Then, you go into a panicked state — a fight or flight battle for your next breath.

Experts state that **there is a "rule of threes" when it comes to the essentials of life**. They state that you can go about three weeks without food, three days without water, three hours without shelter, and three minutes without air. Obviously these guidelines can vary depending on where you live and your own physical condition. The point is, **there are basic essentials we need for survival.**

When it comes to moving from surviving to thriving, we believe there are four laws (essentials needed to thrive) which, like gravity, are continuously shaping our individuality.

> *These four laws act silently upon our individuality. They are **Self Care, Self-Expression, Mastery and Progress**. These four laws directly, quietly and consistently act upon our lives.*

Expressing our individuality, empowers and fuels our Drive to Thrive. We believe our Drive to Thrive is critical to our ability to Fully Inhabit Our Life. It fills and bridges the gaps between surviving and thriving and builds resilience.

So, what builds our resilience and drive to thrive?

> On a physical level, "Is it possible that our emotional reactions and responses affect our body and immunity and wellbeing?" and, "does the body affect our emotions?"

There is a whole biological component to our body that is made up of biological cycles that all are dependent on the other in order for our systems to run efficiently.

Interestingly enough, this linkage includes our nervous system (which is linked to our metabolic processes and hormones, and energy cycles etc.).

> ***Even our emotions and feelings affect our nervous system** and all our body functions. Therefore what we think - affects our feelings, emotions and our nervous system.*

The "Second Brain" influences mood and well-being.

It is known that the the stomach and intestines operate like a second brain. The brain sends messages to the whole body, but the gut also talks back to the brain. So if either of the two are troubled, it affects the other. When you are stressed, your gut knows it immediately. For instance, low levels of serotonin are linked to Irritable Bowel Syndrome, IBS. Plus, gut bacteria affects our eating cravings by acting through the vagus nerve, which connects 100 million neurons from the GI tract to the base of the brain.

Our enteric nervous system produces more than 30 neurotransmitters by the neurons, which line the gut. These produce 95% of the body's serotonin. These neurochemicals are used by the brain to regulate basic body processes as well as the mental processes such as learning, memory and mood. So our stomach influences both mood and the gastrointestinal activity. There are five hundred million neurons in the enteric system, which is 0.5% that in the human brain (80 to 100 billion). There are 100 million neurons in the human spinal cord.

To explain this, 80 to 100 billion neurons are in the brain and only 500 million are found in the gut. However, the neurotransmitters in the brain are essential for function, yet 95% of them are produced in the gut.

For this reason, the balance of different types of bacteria in the gut microbiome affects your emotions and the way your brain processes signals from your senses like sight, sound, flavours and textures.

So a way to increase serotonin naturally in the body is to eat foods with the essential amino acid tryptophan, found in salmon, eggs, spinach, seeds, turkey, milk, soy, nuts. This is where the expression is pertinent - to "feed your brain".

Taking care of the second brain, the GI tract, is essential to keeping the brain healthy so that it can function at its best to have clarity. That way I you are able to learn and adjust to challenges that come your way.

Understanding how the neuroplastic brain is able to function, adapt, grow and learn is a useful way to understand how we think, and the habits and patterns that are deeply entrenched within us.

The second brain is as important as the cerebral brain because they influence the other. Thus the science of neuroplasticity would include the interactions of the two and how they affect the other.

Therefore, you can see how important it is to find an optimal equilibrium between the gut and the brain - that's going to support physical and mental health.

When we learn to leverage the neuroplasticity of the brain, we accelerate our growth, development and sense of well-being.

Your Super-Power: "You CAN Retrain Your Neuroplastic Brain!"

To master your life you **must learn how to master the subconscious activity that influences most of your life**. Becoming aware of it is key. Once you are aware of it, you can change it.

When you begin to be more intentional, you **automatically program or influence the subconscious mind**, making positive shifts toward what serves your highest and best interests. Plus, you will **stop being enslaved to subconscious habitual patterns**.

> *Let's look at how this phenomenon works and how you can apply it, using the latest research and science of neuroplasticity of the brain* ***(and its ability to change).***

When you are under stress, your brain processes thoughts differently. If you are in a state of stress physically or emotionally, the primitive brain instinctively and unconsciously goes into fight or flight mode. This causes your body to produce stress hormones. As well, the more the nerve cells in the primitive brain are used, the stronger the connections are made and the faster we react. Its metaphorically like a muscle, the more you use it, the stronger it becomes. After awhile, you don't even have to be upset for this part of the central brain to be fired. That is because this emotional centre of the brain has established pathways that cause a state of hypervigilance. You are constantly on alert and looking for evidence that you are going to experience something negative. So you don't even have to have any danger imminent for it to be activated. Any reoccurring thought, memory or even positive exciting stimulus, can be interpreted and quickly processed through these pathways.

All this activity is in response to your feelings like joy, calmness, excitement, anger, anxiety, frustration, and happiness.

> *Yes, your mindset affects your body biologically, chemically, physiologically and metabolically.*

Your brain is structurally changed in response to what you think, because of the addition of more nerve cell connections in a region being used. Each time you think about something, the corresponding part of the brain that is responsible for that thought, is stimulated. When this occurs, the nerve cells along those pathways prompt the DNA to produce the products that are necessary to create more or longer nerve cell connections or dendrites. This creates a network of neuron connections that are intertwined like a nest or a safety net.

> *Thus your thoughts are strengthened and amplified in those parts of the brain, whether they are negative or positive. Your body and mind are connected, so when you are stressed, it affects your body and it leads to physical symptoms. The stress from these body symptoms, also affects the brain and how our brain processes the stress.*

For example, the areas of the brain that can be affected, are those responsible for memory, your senses and intuition, forethought, or problem solving. You literally get more of the same type of thoughts and experiences, when you are stressed, over excited, anxious or sad. This is due to the fact that your body is already in a hyper vigilant state.

So what you place your attention on is what you will continue to experience "more of, or, less of". This is why it is important that you understand how the brain works (science), how it works for you (biology) and how you can use that to your advantage.

The most important aspect of the Life Origami's program is what we have discovered in our studies of neuroplasticity. This is the science of the neuroplastic nature of the brain and its ability to change. Our mastering the brain phase of the program, incorporates the use of this neuroplastic nature in our neurofitness program.

It is based on the brains nerve cells ability to grow in response to our senses and how they are stored into memories. The science supports that a person can attach positive emotions to their senses. This affects the long term uptake of memories, and minimizes the function of neural pathways, that are activated when we are under stress. You can replace emotional triggers associated with memories and transform them into those that serve your higher good.

You can meet the challenge to store and retrieve memories, perform tasks, be creative, problem solve and make decisions. This is all based on your understanding of how your brain works when you are feeling stuck and lost.

What really helps is to know that as we age, its important to keep mentally fit. Even at an older age, our brain still has the ability to grow, adjust and alter patterns and connections. Having a healthy brain involves many factors such as nutrition (to feed the brain), exercise, sleep, stress management, and brain-enhancing activities in our lifestyle.

If you do brain-enhancing activities now in your life, and incorporate them into your lifestyle, its a fortress against some of the loss of thinking power you may have as you age. As we get older, we get entrenched into routines and live unconsciously on autopilot, doing what feels normal or comfortable. When we do this, we are bypassing opportunities to make new associations between thoughts and feelings. We reduce our ability to make or retrieve memories because nerve cells atrophy with non-use. If you don't use them, you lose them.

We have learned that when you use all your senses, you are breaking out of everyday routines. So you are deliberately creating new patterns and strong associations between different parts of the brain. Therefore, you can rewire how you think and your experiences in the future. You can strengthen your pathways and connections between various parts of the brain, so that they are working in harmony.

The opportunity here, is that you can access these fit parts of the brain when challenges come up. You can think clearly in order to respond, feel confident, feel calm inside. You have the ability to adapt, learn, grow and cope.

> *The correlation between what you feel, think, and believe should be obvious by now. These along with your emotional reactions, have a key role in your being well or unwell. So you can choose to intentionally learn how to retrain your brain to serve you. Health and wellbeing are created by consistently focusing on your dreams, passions and gratitudes. In addition, focusing on what motivates you and getting on with living your dreams, instead of just dreaming them, builds a life-affirming mindset and builds positive habitual patterns.*

At Life Origami we affirm, that since everything is connected, the path to happiness and a long life is all about having a healthy and intentional mind.

Happiness and Life Longevity

Our longevity has been correlated with how happy a person is over their lifetime. Some nations like Japan have an extremely high life expectancy of individuals living over 100 years old. They attribute this to the fact that their happiness factor is very high.

If a person has fun and is happy and it affects their physical wellbeing, doesn't it make sense then to examine what impacts our well-being?

> *Our feelings, thoughts and belief systems could be negatively impacting our health through the vast network of body systems, nerves and neural connections.*

Old patterns and false beliefs may be affecting our stress levels, which interferes with our ability to find joy daily. This can lead to all types of physical problems like depression, fatigue, stomach ulcers , IBS, etc.

Our emotional disposition also affects our attitudes and behaviours. So the way we think influences our decision making. If we are feeling negative, we may make decisions that sabotage our efforts to be well.

For instance, the decision to not take our health seriously by not exercising or improper nutrition - affects our heart and cardiovascular system. As a result, strokes and heart attacks occur.

If it is true, that the mind affects the body, we need to change our attitude about self care. When we take care of ourselves we feel calmer inside. Being calm is the foundation of our ability to cope with life and helps us thrive (not just survive). Without serenity, we will struggle.

So, what are you doing to fully inhabit **your** life? Are you experiencing at your core, a **foundation of serenity**, day to day? Is your life fun and joyful?

Did you know smiling and laughing can actually extend your life. ;-)

Challenges come at us unexpectedly and quickly. What can we do to prepare ourselves to adapt to various challenges, as they come our way? We need new attitudes, skills and tools to be able to adapt and stand upon a foundation of your own inherent wisdom. This is what you will experience when you begin to become acquainted with your Lost Guru. First, you will need to identify what prevents you from tapping into this inner resource. This is a resource, which has all the key distinctions, insights and wisdom you will ever need to fully inhabit your life. This is The Lost Guru.

2. The Habits, Patterns & Obstacles Preventing You From Accessing Your Greatness

Our greatest support to begin fully inhabiting our lives, lies within us. The first step is to confront an uncomfortable truth:

> *The ultimate crime against ourselves is the **denial of our greatness and our weaknesses.** The cause of this denial is fear, which cuts us off at the junction of our comfort zone and personal growth.*

Everybody has **untapped and undeveloped potential**. We get caught in a loop of embracing our strengths but denying and/or ignoring our weaknesses. We know our strengths and tend to concentrate our attention on them, because its easy and seems to work for us. We give little attention to developing our weaknesses, because that means we have to step out of our comfort zone and step into unknown territory.

*If we are going to transform our weaknesses and embrace our greatness within, we will have to overcome **the fundamental negative belief,** that on some level, **we are... "Not Enough."***

This "Not Enough" belief becomes a story. A story that is so well hidden, even as you read this, you might think that this doesn't apply to you. Wait, keep reading there are all sorts of cloaked behaviours which keep us drinking the "not enough" Kool aid.

We don't allow ourselves to even admit we are thinking we are "not enough." We try to stuff it down, hide it and ignore it. We might have even decided to "fake it, until we make it". This only reinforces the **"not enough" thought virus** and keeps us stuck in the loop of ignoring it. We do not even try to move forward beyond the thought virus loop, and this is how we victimize ourselves. This "not enough" belief is one of the most well disguised and unspoken human secrets.

If we don't confront this fear, we will stay stuck in the fear of the unknown and our progress will be slow or non-existent. We limit ourselves.

When we refuse to admit or identify our greatness, we are indirectly denying the very intellect, genius, and ability we have to make things happen. This has a negative impact on how we think and our self confidence. So then, one or a combination of patterns may present themselves.

First, we may shrink back and adopt a skulker pattern. We begin to think about why we aren't good enough. And this keeps us stuck in the "not enough" loop.

Second, we may take on some of the emulator patterns. When we do this, we pay more attention to our strengths and pretend that our weaknesses don't exist. We pretend we are somebody that we are not. In an attempt to minimize our weaknesses, we do the opposite. We blow our strengths out of proportion; we puff ourselves up to others, and yet, we are still not living from our authentic self.

Thirdly, we may assume the copy cat role. We may model and mimic someone else and take on their personality and lifestyle. This reminds us of the books in the library of Gatsby, in the book called "The Great Gatsby". Gatsby's books in his library, were pretentious; the covers were leather but were blank inside. Gatsby was an emulator and a copy cat. He just tried to impress people with his parties and house. Everything about him was just for show. However, his self esteem was so low that he never showed up for his own parties. In this example, he didn't show up to live his own life, he lived someone else's.

Fourth, we may be caught in a powerful denial pattern. We might be aware of our weaknesses but we don't admit them to to ourselves or others. Plus, we won't let ourselves accept our greatness. We live the life of "Mr/Ms. In-between." We play-it safe and are indecisive, not able to step beyond uncertainty. We live in a rut of self-imposed complacency. This is how we trick ourselves thinking we are doing "good enough", and therefore, we don't need to try something new.

On the other hand, when we step into our power and tell ourselves that we "can-do" something, we bypass our inner critic and change the odds in our favour. To do that, we will need to understand the patterns that keep us trapped in the "not enough" zone.

Understanding The Four Patterns Which Keep Us Trapped In The "Not Enough" Zone

What you are about to read are broad generalizations and tendencies. These are patterns of thinking and behaviours we have observed as people attempt to become more conscious and have control over their lives. Do not fall prey to labelling yourself. Over the course of your lifetime, you have probably experienced or observed many of these patterns and habits in yourself and in others.

We suggest that you highlight those which resonate or you find yourself reacting to. If you feel a a sense of revulsion, anger or tension as you read these four patterns — simply breathe, observe and highlight them. These feelings are blips on the radar screen of your consciousness. Pay attention to them, but remember they are not who you are. They are reactions and behaviours that you have developed over the course of your lifetime.

There is wisdom in those reactions, trust and explore it. Remember, tension seeks resolution. Our reactions are like the tension of a rubber band. The more attention (pull) on the rubber band of your awareness, the more we want to react and pull back.

> *We suggest that you highlight and make notes as you read. Remember, the first step to change is awareness, respect the tension as you read. It is your active witness giving you a helping hand by recognizing the unconscious patterns in your life.*

The Emulator Pattern

One of the core wounds of the emulator pattern, is that they feel like an imposter. They feel this way because they feel like they are living a lie, someone else's life. As well, they have lost sight of their dreams, goals and priorities. They are so focused on keeping others happy that they have lost their bearings. So, they offset this feeling through hard work. They compensate for having weaknesses by becoming obsessed with their strengths. They are many classic over-achievers within this pattern. Some may work so hard that they are bordering on being workaholics. They are constantly in motion, keeping themselves busy. In as much as they attempt to live a balanced life, they struggle to make little time for themselves.

They pride themselves on their ability to get along with anyone. They are the chameleons. They attempt to please and get along, but get caught in the trap of fixing and rescuing others. The key distinction between helping others and fixing others, is that they do this without the other people's permission. They are hyper-vigilant, alert and paying attention to other people's business, judging other people's actions. They feel jealous of other people's success. This is because they secretly doubt their own abilities to reach their full potential.

While growing up they learned to be the "good kid" who did what they were told. Yet, they also ended up assimilating and adopting other people's expectations, opinions and "shoulds". Hidden deep inside is a fundamental sense of insecurity and inferiority. This drives their need for recognition; if they do not get the recognition they desire, they feel incomplete and "not enough." Deep down they want to be authentic and original. They are aware of the need to walk their own walk, but they struggle with it. What prevents them from fully inhabiting their life is their dependence and need for approval and recognition.

When caught in the Emulator pattern, their Inner Critic keeps them trapped in the thinking virus that "I'm Not Enough". In addition, they think, "If I admit my weakness, it confirms that I am bad and not adequate." They deny their greatness because they are afraid of failure. To them failure means they are "not enough".

The Emulator pattern dissipates when the person becomes uncomfortable with the tension between their morals and values. They begin to see, how everything they do, is driven by their need for recognition and control. This is disturbing to them, because they consider themselves to be a "people" person. This is because they were so deeply entrenched in living on auto-pilot, and they lost their way. They are going through the motions of life according to how they think it "should" be. Unfortunately, they may not be living the life that feels significant and meaningful, congruent with their values.

The Denier Pattern

A Denier pattern becomes evident when they refuse to acknowledge they have weaknesses or strengths. They refuse to learn from their life experience even when presented with evidence that they fell short or did well.

They deny in an attempt to deflect reality or the truth, in an effort to control by stuffing it down so they don't have to deal with it or their feelings.

What keeps the Denier trapped, is they have become accustomed to a pattern of listening to their inner critic. When paying homage to their negative self talk, they end up doubting their abilities to live the life they want. So, they hold back and avoid facing reality and dealing with it. In the process, they are denying their potential greatness.

As they were growing up, they took pride in their ability to please other people because then they don't have to deal with living their own lives. They do not take advantage of the opportunities that are presented to them that will foster growth.

When they are heavily involved in this pattern, they are indecisive because they struggle to think for themselves. So they do not make the decisions or choices to support their greater good. They tend to weigh the pros and cons endlessly. This is because they do not want to fail or be "wrong". So, they work hard to make sure they are on the "right side" of an issue or problem. They often find themselves stuck "in-between" people and situations. They are always trying to mend fences and keep everybody happy. They often change their minds to please others or keep things "safe". As a result, they can appear kind of wishy washy. This is because they tend to flip flop between all the opinions of others.

When basking in the denier pattern, they wrap themselves in a blanket of "smiles, positivity and excessive people pleasing". This actually is masking the fear that they are "not enough". We often are deceived by these facades and have no idea these people are struggling. There are even times that we hear of someone committing suicide, and we feel shocked because we considered them to be very "happy, social, and all-together."

The biggest wound of the Denier pattern is how they miss out on their own life. They become so concerned about making the wrong decisions; they easily end up in analysis paralysis. On the other hand, when feeling frustrated or anxious, they can swing in the opposite direction and make impulsive decisions. This is the paradox of the Denier pattern. On one hand they appear very deliberate and careful, and then surprise you with an impulsive decision or action. These swings occur because of the confusion of what they want or need to do, when compared to other people's expectations.

This leaves them lost because they question themselves and don't trust in their own efficacy. So they sit on the frozen fence of indecision in situations like relationships, in fear of change and the unknown. They are like puppets on the strings of other people's agendas. This tempts them to maintain bad or toxic relationships at work, home and in the community.

They also get trapped in denial, due to a false sense of confidence. They think, "Things aren't that bad." As a result, this Pollyanna attitude keeps them from seeing things as they are. Then they miss out on key lessons, distinctions and learning opportunities.

In the Denier pattern, a person learns to accept a perpetual state of uncertainty. So, in an attempt to "not be wrong", they are always riding the fine line of other people's opinions. As a result, they remain stuck "in-between" reality and the life they wish they had.

They wake up when they can't cope with life events. They blame their current circumstances on their indecisiveness. They obsess over what could have been said or done. Instead, they could have just chosen to get on with living life, to the best of their abilities.

The Skulker Pattern

The skulker patterns evolve due to experiencing a lot of criticism (from self or others) in their lifetime. People who exhibit these patterns may become aware of weaknesses to the point where they obsess over them. So they deny their greatness, because their attention to their weaknesses trumps looking at their good features.

Therefore, they tend to indulge in story telling and justification as to why they are the way they are. This obsessive need to cling to their stories, creates a lot of stinking thinking involving blame, shame and guilt. They cope, albeit ineffectively, by bottling up their feelings, turtling and hiding from themselves and others. They have this persistent pressure or low-lying undertone of anxiety always present beneath the surface of their awareness. The really don't know this is happening because they have done such a good job of trying to bury it. Prolonged anxiety can develop into many types of physiological ailments and psychological symptoms. That's where depression, high blood pressure, immunity dysfunctions, weight gain (to list a few) can present themselves. This causes further stress on the body and a biofeedback loop occurs, of stress feeding more stress.

In the presence of negative self-talk, some people may become anti-social, self-involved, shut-ins or home bodies. They tend to carry a lot of unresolved tension which may cause anger management issues.

Skulkers may not trust others because they fret over how they will be treated by others. This is because they don't feel like they are enough. So they may end up playing the people pleaser role within relationships. All of this happens because they chase approval externally rather than internally. As a result, they end up denying themselves and their potential for greatness.

They don't feel like they are enough, and they think they have a lot to work on. Therefore, they are on a constant quest of self-improvement. They are heavily invested in books, seminars/webinars and the personal development industry.

When someone is locked in the Skulker Pattern, they tend to live in a perpetual survival mode. They never really arrive at a level of inner peace, because they are constantly tearing themselves apart.

They finally wake up when they hit the bottom of the blame, shame and guilt barrel. When they become aware, despite all their hard work and things aren't working, they realize something needs to change so that they can get what they want. Sometimes it takes becoming exhausted and burned out in order to make the big decisions to create movement in their lives.

The Copy Cat Pattern

People exhibiting a copy cat pattern also tend to be impulsive. They tend to be seen as fickle, demanding and unfocused.

Copy Cats are aware of their weaknesses and they do not think they need to do anything about it, because they are going to be great "damn it". They are convinced that their success is dependent upon how well they model someone else's strategies and tactics. Unfortunately, this can result in a significant inferiority complex, which causes them to continue the "great cover-up". The subtle distinction between the denier and the copy cat, is the copy cat thinks they have the answer to their weaknesses. They try to model someone else and therefore they think they do not have a problem. On the other hand, the denier just doesn't even bother, they are in denial.

The copy cat pattern involves the belief that everyone else has their answers. So they model and copy other people that they deem to be successful. They think they will become great too, which will make their weaknesses moot.

They engage in the personal development industry and have bought into the teachings of some other guru, in the context of that guru's life. They do not trust in the wisdom of their own life, because they do not trust themselves. They follow the old adage of "Fake it until you make it". They persist at trying to fake it until they can figure out how to become the person that they have idealized. They figure if they play the charade, somehow it will "catch up" with them and they will have become the model of their fantasies.

They do not have many original ideas, and when they do, they don't trust them enough and have learned to focus on other people's ideas and opinions. They wear the persona until they implode from the pain of their lack of authenticity. They get trapped in being part of the in-crowd, and many people see them as leaders. However, they are experiencing the opposite of that as long as they are followers.

The Inner Critic of a Copy Cat pattern, keeps them trapped in the thinking virus that "everyone else is more credible and lovable than I am."

They wake up when they realize that for all that they've done, to mimic and model other people, it hasn't produced the quality life they thought. At some point, they begin to experiment with their own ideas, and discover that they have more potential than they thought. They begin to speak up for what they believe in, despite potential consequences. When they finally realize that the Copy Cat lifestyle is not getting them what they want, they begin to explore what they think and want in life.

It doesn't matter whether you resonate with the Emulator, Denier, Skulker or Copy cat patterns (or combination thereof), these patterns are not who you are. Whatever patterns are playing out in your life, the tension you may have felt, while reading these descriptions, are indicators of your tension patterns. These **tension patterns** represent an opportunity for you to gain insights, learn and expand your capabilities.

Tension Is (Actually) Your Friend

Tension, like stress, is something we avoid and have been taught is "bad" for us. What if tension is actually your friend? If this were true, then you would be working to have a healthy relationship with it, right?

Guess what? Tension by its nature seeks resolution. It is this fundamental principle that embodies the greatest quality of a friend. Think about it this way - a good friend will confront you when they think you are making a mistake. They will give you honest, unbiased feedback. Tension operates the same way. Tension, always has your best interest at heart. Why? It is an inherent and natural part of the creative process. Living, aging and moving through life itself is a creative act.

Understand, tension is a normal part of life. However, we tend to ignore tension because we have been conditioned to resist it. It is important to mention that tension is the catalyst for all change in our habitual patterns.

Therefore, to make a shift in our habits we first need awareness. Rather than stuff and ignore or avoid the tension, we need to stay with it long enough to extract the insight and/or direction inherent in the energy we feel. When we make the shift to view tension as our friend, a remarkable transformation occurs.

We begin to see that when we feel tension, it is an early warning signal that change is due. Think of it like an x-ray, that shows you what lies beneath the surface of your skin. Therefore, tension is your body's intelligence attempting to get your attention.

We are not suggesting that tension is something you should go looking for. Tension is simply a natural outcome or consequence that rises from an intention to grow and expand.

The very fact that you hold an intent to change, to expand and become more — creates this tension. Tension is explained as being present when there are opposing energies, between your existing state and a desired future state.

So the fact that we experience tension isn't the problem. Rather, tension is simply contrast, which is created as a result of choosing to become more. Setting an intention to "change" gives birth to a state, that is translated into "creative tension". This creates the energy we feel and subsequently label as tension. Tension always precedes every single creative act from our cave man days to today. Tension is simply the rising physiological energy and when we take action, it becomes the expression or release of this "creative energy".

So the next time you feel tension, try this experiment. Make friends with this creative energy and follow the flow. When you do, you will be open and able to recognize how tension might be an indicator of an opportunity. The key is to be open to learning from it. Resist the urge to deny, avoid or stuff the tension down, acknowledge it, explore and embrace it. When you learn to master tension, you also learn how to work with it, to express yourself and uncover your greatness.

Self Expression Takes a Nose Dive When We Deny Our Greatness

It is always easier to deny, avoid and ignore our greatness. We stay in denial because we can't look the truth in the eye. We would have to get in touch with our gritty, messy truth — that **we don't truly believe in ourselves** and we are holding ourselves back. Its just easier to say, "I'm not capable, there's no potential", than to admit our hand in our circumstances."

> *When this happens, we lose **intimacy with ourselves and our dreams**; as well, we lose **intimacy with others**. When we cross our*

> ***self-integrity line**, we **dishonour ourselves.** We are **denying our divinity** and **our existence**.*

More often then not, the crime of shrinking back from our greatness and true potential, is empowered by our subconscious beliefs. These are a byproduct of the meaning we assign to our past experiences and our inaccurate memories.

The Wet Blanket of Inaccurate Memories

Many of these beliefs and our self-doubt are all wrapped up in a **wet blanket of past experiences** and memories. Each one of us has a repertoire of **confused facts** somewhere in our memories. We have attachments to **incomplete and inaccurate stories** in our mind. These vague memories from our past, are based on our limited understanding of the full context of the circumstances at that time. In the past, without this understanding, we may not have made congruent decisions. Either that or we skirted around and were indecisive for whatever reasons. Often we allow our memories to go by unchallenged. Because so much time has passed, we may be stuck in our old belief systems and have warped perspectives.

Time-warped Memories and Decision Making

So, not only do our memories fade and elude us over time, so do the facts. We can't recount the actual events in the manner they happened because it was so long ago.

> *When we have a warped memory, the same emotions that were experienced at the time, are trapped within us. When that happens, our imagination tends to blow things out of proportion.*

We might still identify with those past feelings, attitudes and payoff-excuses. We end up thinking something happened in a way that didn't. Our story distorts the truth of what actually happened. When our emotions run rampant, **we come to believe in our own stories**. These become malignant lies that we tell ourselves, and they grow like a fisherman's tale over time. This is because, believing in our stories is easier than confronting the past and facing the fact that we stayed ambivalent.

The problem with ambivalence is that it keeps us tied down in self-doubt and long term trust issues. This is because we didn't make the decisions that could have changed our lives.

We need to have good outcomes when we make decisions, which creates confidence. When this happens, we feel empowered to make the right decisions, at the right time, for the right reason. And then it is easier to step into our greatness with a strong foundation of self-trust and self-acceptance.

So confronting and examining our memories and our decision making skills, gives us a lot of insight into what has shaped us today. It also points our awareness that there is an opportunity to grow.

> *Decision making becomes more solid and congruent when we know what we want in life and who we are. This can happen when we understand our strengths and weaknesses and how to work with them.*

This awareness fuels using our gifts and talents; self-expression flowers and grows. **Self-expression is an invaluable tool for creating momentum in our lives.** This is what brings meaning, empowerment and significance to us. Unless, we get caught in a cycle of performance based acceptance.

Performance Based Acceptance Is A Toxic Thought Virus

We get taught to perform for acceptance by our parents and family, friends, school system, society and our employers. Then, we begin to pursue approval from others and learn to adjust our behaviour, to ensure we get that approval. When this happens, we have entered into a "feel good presence" and pattern of behaviour called, "**performance based acceptance.**"

This Performance Based Acceptance (PBA) occurs when we **rely on the opinions and favourable approval of others, *instead* of our own.** We seek love and acceptance, but we settle for Performance Based Acceptance as a **substitute for self-love and self-acceptance**. The problem with this is that it becomes a persistent, unconscious, and engrained habit. Plus, it creates an identity crisis within us. When this happens, we **allow other people's approval to overshadow or even supersede our own opinions and perspectives.**

As a child, the cycle of PBA begins when we first internalize positive feedback like "aren't you a **good boy/girl!**" In school we immediately notice how we get more positive affirmations and acceptance when we get a grade of A versus an F or D. Or the teachers say, "good boys and good girls don't interrupt the teacher, they put their hand up". And the person who puts their hand up gets the teachers attention, love and praise. And the kid who speaks up rather than putting their hand up, is asked to be quiet and not interrupt the other kids (even though their input might be more pertinent).

When we go shopping with our parents, we are told to "behave ourselves ... if you are a good girl/boy, I'll buy you a cookie." Or when a mother takes her young son shopping for patterns and fabric, he hears the words, "be a good boy ... be quiet while I do this." Or we have often heard, "Children should be seen and not heard."

> *But the problem is,* ***the quiet kid is not heard and gets less attention and love.*** *They learn to perform for approval by getting attention.*

Often the kids end up acting out by trying to get their "good little boy/girl hero cookies" for the love and acceptance they crave. Here are a few scenarios where we have observed performance based acceptance occurring.

For example, when we grow up and want to go to college, our parents may say we should not go because we aren't smart enough. Somehow C's in high school aren't good enough for the parents, even though they might get us into college or a trade school. Our parents may say that we shouldn't go to college, because mother's should "stay home with their kids and not neglect them", having someone else raise them. We may also hear comments that indicate we should become an doctor, engineer, computer analyst or nurse — because artists, actresses, comedians or musicians don't earn enough money. When we change our behaviour, to appease others, do we get the hero cookies that we crave?

Parents who believe in fortune-telling and complain that if their kids want to be an artist, they will end up on the streets begging for money. Whether this becomes a short term reality or not, the point is that if we believe these words, we don't even try to do great things, make decisions based on our own preferences, or go after our dreams. We stop following what we love because we are performing for others acceptance. We **end up just giving into the expectations and "shoulds" of other people.**

Another example may be when we are compared to an older sibling. In this case it depends on who the "golden child" is for the moment, and doing everything just "right".

In the workplace, our boss praises our performance, because we anticipate what everybody wants without being asked. So we end up becoming everybody else's "Girl Friday" (aka water-boy).

Where this becomes a huge issue is when this performance based acceptance (PBA) becomes a part of our identity. We slowly ***become reliant on other people's approval.*** *We come to* ***crave acceptance*** *and kudos because it makes up for our low self-esteem.*

It is true that what makes the world go around is people helping people. The difference between helping people and PBA is permission. When we have someone else's permission to help them, we are working on something together.

When we are anticipating what people need, and then performing to get their approval and acceptance by helping them, essentially we are volunteering to fix them (without their permission).

When this is successful, we get caught up in the PBA merry-go-round where we are jumping off the playground ride of our own life, and jumping onto the slide of someone else's priorities. We hijack our needs and priorities for their approval and agendas. This PBA ends up in a cycle, that everyone engages in, because we are all raised with similar societal messaging and limits. So we become **"others-oriented" and followers**, rather than leaders; we hide behind masks and our originality is not apparently obvious.

So ***if we don't learn to step outside of the PBA cycle*** *and break away from it, momentum is difficult to build and maintain.*

We can end up surrendering our dreams, desires and priorities. We trade them in for others' approval. The problem is, each time we do that, a piece of our pride and self-esteem dies. Eventually our self-esteem and self-confidence needs to be rebuilt.

> *Without self-acceptance there is no confidence to go and pursue what we want.*

Without self-confidence in our own efficacy, we will remain stuck in fear and PBA. It becomes much easier to remain within the comfort zone of our PBA habits. Then we fall into a pattern of resistance to try something new, bold and different.

The good news is, now that you are aware of your PBA tendencies, you can change. Unless you are also trapped on the treadmill of negativity.

The Payoff Of Negativity

When we indulge in negativity from past hurts, the pain and trauma may persist, because there is a payoff for staying in trauma. The payoff is that we **don't have to be accountable or responsible**. It is said that we can't change if we don't admit there's a problem. And a lot of people will fight to the bitter end to avoid this. We have to **step out of our comfort zone and enter the learning curve**.

> *We have to accept the reality that* ***we cannot experience what we aren't willing to confront, examine, release and embrace***.

Confronting is a challenge because we'd have to admit we held ourselves back in the past. And in the present, we still might be. We might discover that our past inaction and indecisiveness, caused us to miss out on the good stuff. It is challenging to realize that we flogged ourselves with old patterns of blame, shame, and guilt-trip beatings, which held us back. We find it hard to confront our past, because we are afraid of feeling the strong emotions that accompanied those negative experiences. We know that part of confronting our truths naturally results in self-responsibility. Then self-accountability looks us in the eye and we know we have to grow up.

Making Decisions

Its quite a big deal how we make decisions and how we feel about our results from the past. **Self recrimination undermines our ability to make decisions; we become indecisive.** And this makes or breaks our ability to get what we want.

The paradox of choice plays a big part in our indecisiveness. Meaning, we can't decide between the multitude of choices out in the world. Two things happen. First, we procrastinate not knowing what to do, and we miss out on opportunities. We talk ourselves out of forward movement, based on the negative projections and judgments going on in our heads. And second, we may have indulged in ambivalence for so long that we don't trust ourselves. When we don't have faith in our own ability to make smart decisions, we panic. We jump onto any horse or cart going into town. We **make rash decisions** because of our fear of missing out. And the interesting thing is that we cannot make congruent decisions if we haven't identified what we want first.

With so many choices, we can get confused as to which one suits our situation best. We can become overly committed to something we end up regretting. The risk of making a impulsive decision can leave us stuck in something that is hard to get out of.

> *The fear that leaves us in stasis is: We are afraid of doing the wrong thing at the wrong time for the wrong reason, and being stuck or hurt in the wrong situation.*

This fear of making bad decisions causes us to second guess ourselves, and we indulge in negative self talk, gutter talk.

Fears and Gutter Talk

Fear is a result of our **negative inner dialogue** and our automatic thoughts, that occur in a split second. The thoughts we listen to between our ears impacts us. We may be listening to our damaged egos that are laden with societal beliefs. We compare ourselves to others and say that we haven't done anything of value, and aren't capable like others. We believe we aren't deserving.

Fear speaks into everyone's lives. Fear is the leading cause of the ultimate crime of denying our weaknesses and our greatness. We fear that we are not enough.

Consider this, "What if fear doesn't actually exist because it's a machination?" Its an imagined, assimilated belief, that doesn't come to fruition just because it worries us.

> ***Worrying holds no magic! Worrying doesn't make bad things happen to you and it doesn't make things better either.***

Fear is defined as: taking your past stories of feeling "Not Enough", and adding them to your present imagination, and projecting drama into the future. Fear is not real, its just an obscure concept that sometimes deters us. Fear is projection and a judgment that something catastrophic could happen. The side effects of fear may be evident, as they affect our body and mind, but fear doesn't make imagined catastrophes real. It gets in the way of our ability to make rational, congruent decisions.

So if this resonates with you, if you've gained an insight into how fear has become a mask that you've been hiding behind, take heart. You are not alone. This is a **common human experience**, and we invite you to open up to how you might escape this way of living. Keep reading with an open mind.

Fear Cuts Off Your Oxygen

You are just punishing yourself when you give into the fear of failure. You are letting it run your life when you allow this to happen, an uncomfortable tension arises.

What happens when you feel tension, is you become afraid of it. When you feel tension, you tend to want to ignore it and stuff it down. When you do this, tension becomes an obstacle to you.

Fear is an obstacle.

When you don't allow yourself the freedom to self-express, its like you are denying yourself the oxygen of life, the very thing you need to thrive. You struggle to be your unique self, and being able to fully inhabit your life is just out of reach.

Sadly, you are living a life that **isn't consistent with your hearts desires**, capabilities and potential.

Here is the subtle distinction - when you aren't aware of your need for self expression, you miss out. You end up missing out on meaningful and significant life experiences. Plus, you do not experience the success of living the dreams you imagined.

When we face a crisis, fear or significant anxiety, we tend to deny what is happening. When your ego is determined to be right, your memories become altered from what really happened, to the version your ego is attached to. When this happens, you can end up rebelling against your own memories, thoughts, emotions, and even the actions you took. Sometimes, we alter them to **conveniently suit** our low self-esteem and match our self-image.

In fact we can deny any occurrence and any form of self-expression. We do this when we say, "Nope. That didn't happen, that's not on me. I'm not really that good at anything. I don't deserve any better. I can't do this." We become addicted to avoidance, and procrastination (coping mechanisms due to fear), which keeps us from getting in touch with our true identity.

Why Your True Identity Is Hidden

Your true identity will remain elusive if you don't learn how to convert your weaknesses (undeveloped potential) into strengths. This is why you often feel your full potential is just out of your reach. This requires knowing yourself on a whole new level. Then you will make congruent decisions to support yourself. You need to know about all aspects of your true nature. This requires learning to tap into your inherent wisdom and experience, not a fictitious facade.

You can't get what you want if you live according to everyone else's rules. If you do this, the lie of your life grows like Pinocchio's nose. Your life gets controlled by others, like a puppet on a string. You never get to be the puppeteer. You end up feeling like an imposter because you don't recognize who you are anymore.

You get all dressed up and hide behind the mask and costume of "Everything is fine thank you very much". You don't allow others to see whats behind the persistent, pretend smile plastered on your face. You don't let your guard down or let others see the real you. You may be so attached to your manufactured persona that you "are not enough". You work overtime to hide your flaws. You are afraid that if people knew the real you, they would figure out that you really are not who you present yourself to be. If other people discovered who you really are, you would be exposed, it would confirm your greatest fear, that you are not enough.

> *So what do you do?* ***Unless you choose to face-up to the truth****, that you* ***are*** *enough, you will have no choice but to continue to disconnect and numb out. You will continue to dodge getting "found out" and fear will run your life. To admit you are holding yourself back, would mean confronting the way you take yourself out of the game. As a result, this would require a significant amount of self-accountability and honesty. Change would be necessary, despite stepping into the unknown. When you are a slave to your fears, it keeps you from reaching your true potential.*

Fear of Mistakes and Failure

When you are afraid of making mistakes, its because you want to avoid failure or repercussions from others. Avoiding failure seems like an intelligent thing to do except it isn't. This is because you miss the learning opportunities that are inherent in so-called failures. The reason you fear failure is because you don't **understand that there is no achievement without the lessons derived through the process of failing.** When there is failure, there is an opportunity to gain an insight and extract a lesson from what happened.

When you are stuck in the fear of failure its because of how you think of it.

> *You have been taught that failure is bad, not good, or that you "don't cut the mustard." But actually,* ***failure is simply feedback without judgment.***

If you can be the observer without all the judgment and blame, you can learn to see the gaps. With the gaps in full view there's an "ah hah" moment and you have insight into how or where you can **change to achieve your outcome**.

What ends up happening is you allow your fears and judgments to take you out. You also miss the greatest opportunity of all, to **extract the lesson from life's feedback**.

The Fear Of Missing Out (FOMO)

The Fear Of Missing Out (FOMO) is an **omnipresent social anxiety**.

> *When you are afraid you may miss out on an opportunity, you could jump into making decisions without using forethought. So that you do not miss out on some benefit or satisfying event, you may end*

up making rash decisions. This is anxiety, which if you are not aware of it, will lead to feeling unsettled, edgy and eventually panicky.

We make rash decisions when we fear that we had better make a decision now, or we will miss out. Your confidence becomes undermined, you doubt your ability to make congruent decisions. Then from that point forward your behaviour is coloured.

The underlying root of FOMO is based on how you are thinking about yourself and your self-efficacy. It's about whether you believe you can create a desired or intended result in your life.

There are so many options to choose from in life. You first have to **believe in yourself** so you can make the right decisions.

Indecisiveness comes in to play when you don't trust in your ability to make those decisions. You don't know how to decide what the best option is, because you **don't understand the implications or opportunities**. So what happens is you are afraid of missing out, being different or rocking the boat. You judge yourself when things don't work out or believe it was the wrong decision. You become afraid of making the wrong decision, at the wrong time, for the wrong reason.

In an effort to limit poor judgment, you sit at your ***procrastination window****, waiting for another opportunity, or you do nothing and thereby think you are avoiding failure.*

Some people work hard to get somewhere and then when they actually do, it scares them. Remember, if you don't know what you want and what your intentions are, then everything you do could lead you down a path which lands you where you do not want to be. It is like you are shooting in the dark without knowing where the target is. This only serves to heap more anxiety on the pile. Over the long term, when you stay in a state of unease, you can lose confidence in your ability to exercise control over your life.

Procrastination becomes your lazy beer buddy at the bar of complacency. So, you refuse to risk trying something new, without guarantee of success. This is an **insidious form of self-righteous fear**, wrapped in a blanket of justification, called perfectionism. Perfectionism and procrastination are really good beer buddies. However, they aren't real friends, just substitutes. They each vindicate and justify the other's inaction. It doesn't have to be that way.

You owe it to yourself to develop your personal assets and to build your life. Its a self-responsibility that awakens the hero in all of us - to **develop and recognize our potential**, and reach a higher level of self-awareness.

We invite you to consider that there is an **opportunity to move from simply surviving to actual thriving** — this will require that you release your attachment to "The Stories" you tell yourself.

Attachment To Your Stories

Your identity is made up of all the stories you have been accumulating over your lifetime. When you have a story that you are attached to, based on how your beliefs have evolved, you tend to identify with that story "Me. That's me!"

When you tell yourself that you "aren't enough", and say "that's me", it becomes who you think you are. As a result, you may not even try to make things happen. This is because you are **attached to your identity**, based on those old stories that you have been telling yourself for years, decades or for an entire lifetime. Your identity, based on those old stories have hijacked your life.

> *You think "why bother" and you take yourself out of the game because you don't feel worthy.*

It is **easier to believe "the story" and hide** within it than it is to do the work to overcome it. Then, you would have to face the fear head on and look at how you have judged and condemned yourself. As a result of these judgements, you have unknowingly created a **negative identity**.

> *The irony is that if you don't do the work to overcome these stories, you end up paying a perpetual price of not living your dreams.*

When you create a negative identity, you adopt a belief that you aren't smart enough, rich enough, brave enough, not deserving, or anything else which makes you feel like "I am not enough".

So you may sabotage your own efforts and absorb a subtle **unconscious code of negligence.** This code clouds how you see yourself. You end up disregarding your true nature and the essence of your need for self-expression. When that happens, you don't even try to develop your potential and chase your dreams (you let them die).

> *Once you detect that you are not living according to your own standards, you have a choice to make. You either stuff it down and ignore it again. Or, you look in the mirror and choose to embark on a process of self enquiry, to determine if they are your own standards, or ones you have adopted.*

In our experience, it is always a **best practice to examine** the root of your emotions, of feeling like you are not enough or even worthlessness. When you confront your "not enough" feelings, you are less likely to abandon your dreams and hold back from the opportunity to fully inhabit your life.

> *When you know the difference between others standards and your own, you can regain control.*

You regain control because you now are bringing your standards into your conscious awareness. Through a process of enquiry and examination, those feelings of tyranny and pain are exposed. This provides an opportunity to **stop clinging** to those feelings and memories. This is important because they are diverting you from living your life with personal integrity and confidence.

At some point, you can decide to **summon the courage to challenge** some of our deep assumptions from your childhood. Self-destructive patterns and negative habits are often given birth throughout our childhood. Challenging your parents values and choosing to consciously adopt or reject them, is also a necessary part of growing up and becoming your own person.

Like all children, you may have worried about a multitude of things. Then, those fears followed you into adulthood. If you can confront and challenge those fears, then you can discover the "Real You" and expose the real "Not You!"

Be Willing & Ready To Learn, Change and Grow

Like every other member of the human race, your primary years shaped who you are today. As a child it is natural then that we end up adopting our parents point-of-view. Its normal. You were doing what you needed to do to learn, grow and move forward in life. Yet, you can still end up feeling lost and confused.

As teenagers, you may have rebelled against your parents as you were claiming your independence. You were in resistance to your parents values, and wanting to be your own person. However, this resistance adds to the complexity of your learning curve. You may not be able to enter the learning curve to resolve these issues until many years later, perhaps now is the time. The uncomfortable truth is you carry these insecurities and false identities into adulthood.

You spend a lifetime trying to find out who you are and what you are made of, where you want to go. This presents another dilemma of — how are you going to get there?

You don't have to feel bad for wanting to live your own life and feel good.

You will have to figure out how to cross the bridge of the new awareness, that it will take some conscious effort and work to experience the new you.

Then, you have to figure out how you are going to get there.

If anything is going to be different, you have to be willing to learn and change. This can only happen when you **face your fears and do something different** than what you've always done.

This means **being willing to learn and change** and question the validity of your memories. Gaps in the old memories of pain and trauma inhibits real progress. Some of those memories may not be accurate because they were so long ago. Memories can be distorted by your flawed insecurities, emotions and the imagination of a much younger and immature you.

In our experience, when you examine your past, it will give you insight into how it has shaped you.

Honouring Yourself

When you are ready to honour your needs, desires, and rights to self-expression, you might be afraid of the repercussions.

If you are going to live by your own standards, this is the point of no return.

When you are afraid of the consequences of a decision, based on your own standards, you are letting fear control you. If you fail to adopt your own standards and beliefs, you run the risk of never getting in touch with the true you. You do this when you indulge in negative self talk and worry. For example, you may worry about something like, "If I make this decision to go my own way, my family will disinherit me and kick me off the family tree."

It takes a lot of courage to go against the familial grain and put your independence ahead of others agendas for your life. You have to choose to stand on your own two feet. This may mean abandoning your reliance for their emotional, financial or spiritual support. Until you examine and consciously choose your own beliefs, values, morals and ethics, you will struggle to fully inhabit your life.

> *When is it going to be a good time to plant your own garden and stop waiting for someone to bring you flowers?*

You are the one that you can count on; **you are the only one who knows the full context of your life,** and that will follow you all the way to your final curtain call.

Don't waste your life on other people's opinions and values, whose personal experiences are irrelevant to yours.

> *You are your own unique being and nobody else can do you better than you. So follow your bliss and don't hold back.*

Follow what you feel passionate about and what makes you feel joyful. Follow your creativity and the F.U.N. factor, and you can't go wrong. You can live a peaceful, serene and creative existence, when you make a conscious choice to discover your lost guru and Fully Inhabit YOUR Life.

3. Growing And Learning Together In Relationships - By Amethyst

We believe that growing and learning together is our highest calling in relationships. This applies whether you are single, in an intimate relationship with a spouse, life partner, business partner or co-worker. We all learn and grow together or we sink together.

> Everyone must partner with others at certain points in life. None of us get through this life without a little "help from our friends". Having heartfelt connections with others, is a primary driving force to fully inhabiting your life. You owe it to yourself to see what you might discover and learn about yourself through the lens of "relationships".

Celebrating Our Individuality Through Self-Expression

Greg and I have been in business together (Life Origami Corporation), for 2 years almost. We bring decades of business and life experience to this new venture. We are not perfect, we are human beings. Like anyone else, we have challenges, feelings, emotions, and a background of diverse experiences. But the golden thread is we are each **engaged within our own learning curves**. We have extracted the lessons from life's ups and downs and with that perspective, have a better sense of what's important to us today. We know what works now, and what hasn't in the past.

We know who we are as individuals, which has manifested a more present, connected relationship. As a result, we feel confident, enthusiastic and able to still engage in our own unique style of self-expression.

Greg and I are very alike in many ways. Quite noticeably at times, we also are different. However, I appreciate these differences and find that we thrive because we can just be ourselves. And I also wake up each day knowing I'm **free to express my creativity**. I can just "be" and follow my muse; Greg is usually right behind me doing his own thing, or us doing it together.

As individuals, Greg and I **know what we want in life** and what makes it meaningful and significant. As a couple, we also know what we want to **experience together** too. So we try to live with all this in mind. We pretty much do things together and make decisions together.

Best Partners, in Business and Life

I would like to tell you that it has been one of the **best business experiences of my life** working with Greg at Life Origami. I have owned various business but never had a business partner to co-create with. I have had numerous employees and worked with numerous colleagues, scientists, entrepreneurs, technicians, professors, managers, and artists. However, my best experience is working with Greg, my husband and business partner.

Let me explain why.

Collaboration and Harmony

When Greg was my business coach in 2006 to 2007, we worked very well together to get my business developed and operating. I knew his business style. So when we got re-connected in 2017 and married, we were always researching and talking about what we learned in life and business. I was aware of his ethical and moral convictions way back in 2006/07, and they continued to evolve. He has even **more insights as to why life and business can't exist separate from the other.** So I knew he would make a good business partner, as we are both of the same frame of mind. A year later after marrying, we were able to come together to form the Life

Origami Corporation. This is possible because we work so well together, in so many ways.

Connection and Communication

We have a great connection. Therefore, whenever we become emotional and disagreements arise, whether in life or business, we are able to come to a solution successfully. Here is the trick, **we fully discuss the problems until we both feel emotionally connected**. This only happens when we have spoken our full truths and not withheld.

Like most couples, problems are inter-mixed with many other thoughts, to the point that our challenges become complex. This is because our feelings and emotions in business and life are all connected together. Since we each trust the other, we can share our feelings, without fixing or rescuing the other. **We each take responsibility for our own mental wellbeing.** This includes how we deal with our emotions and behaviour before, during, and after speaking together. Sometimes we each need to process our thoughts on our own. So we take time to journal or get some fresh air when necessary. Then, we always come together to discuss it as soon as possible.

We have a physical book with real paper (not an application on the computer or device) — its more kinaesthetic to write in a physical paper journal (i.e. holistic mind/body connection). This journal is where we express gratitude for one another. Its not a problems journal, its a gratitudes journal. We also have our own individual journals.

Sometimes when we have challenges, we light a candle, what we named our "presence" candle. Our purpose for this is to let the other know we are okay, while we are processing thoughts. And it also means there is no need for alarm. A few times I had to light the candle while Greg was coaching. I had some bad news about my dog, I needed to go for a walk — I lit the candle. When he was finished coaching, he could see the candle and know everything was okay. When I returned he was available to talk. If

I am very disturbed or ill, I let him know and wait for him to finish the coaching call. Usually we don't have to go to the extreme to light the presence candle. We generally get onto things right away as they come up. Sometimes though, we may need to think through personal issues before we begin to dialogue. This way we can talk about things, without personal emotional confusion or unresolved baggage. We do discuss these issues as well and because we have done our own processing, we don't project on the other. Then, we talk it through until we feel all is well again and we are emotionally connected.

> *We show up for one another, and* ***we don't shut the other out****. We are a strong loving couple because we don't hold back from the other.*

I won't use the words "a strong TEAM" to describe us because I have issues with it. For such a loving relationship, it just seems too utilitarian. Rather, we are both passionate about being together in whatever we do.

> *We are* ***each fully inhabiting our lives*** *on this journey, along side of one another.*
>
> *Our motto is* ***"Loving Life and Learning Together"****. And for us, it is so true.*

Keeping Our Relationship Clean

Our business is an extension of our congruency and connection as a couple. Our life reaches into our business too. We **maintain harmony in our relationship**, and as a result, don't feel tension around when to work or when to take time off. With a new corporation, there is a lot of work to be done and sometimes requires longer hours. What we do — is agree on our workflow, priorities and schedules. Most times we work side by side on the projects. Sometimes the work flow goes better if we follow our individual muse and then come back together to collaborate.

Talking It Out

So we are learning the ins and outs of being together. If there is a tension between the two of us for whatever reason, we deal with it rather than hold it in. Sometimes I am not aware I'm upset. When I notice that my body hurts or I feel tense, I know there's something up, and I take time to think about what's bothering me. Sometimes we will light our presence candle and create sacred time to talk. That is a reminder for us that devices are to be put away and/or notifications turned off. It makes it easier to discuss our innermost thoughts and feelings because we are not distracted by our devices and we are able to maintain our connection. Which is why our couple **and** individual time is so important to us.

Time Management

When we first began writing, we would divide up work. Then the other would critique, add additional commentary, and edit the article for grammar and punctuation. Neither of us had the full context of what the other was thinking and speaking to, while writing. We realized we spent more time explaining, catching up and editing, which caused our productivity to suffer. We decided to make a change to our work flow.

Many times, our clients comment that Greg and I make a great tag team/ couple. I can relate to this because when we work together we produce our best work. When **we brain storm, our ideas fuel one another** and our work goes in a new, vibrant direction. Not only has the quality of our work improved, but it enhances our strong connection. When we work together on a project, not only does our **passion increase, there is also less tension**. We do not feel a tension or any time pressure because there no longer a need to explain what we worked on, and rebuild our connection and flow as a couple. Then, when our work is completed, we have more personal time together or time to ourselves.

We don't work all day and rarely week-ends. Some days we work half days, depends on our coaching or video production schedule. Working side by side makes it is so much easier to make decisions. If we have to purchase new supplies, apps and paying for business bills and wages, we do it all together. Greg handles the business taxes, deductions and wages. But we work together on the rest. I maintain the spreadsheets for life and business because I love the challenge. I enjoy the math and analytical stuff in spreadsheets. Greg had to do all that work, years before I came along, so its a nice break for him. We make a great team in business and in our home life.

Down Time

There are many things we do to **take breaks throughout the day**, to support our individual energy and work time preferences. Generally we wake up early and have coffee/tea together, no work related discussions (most days). After we talk, we go up to the writing and coaching room where the whiteboards are. We brain storm, make mind maps, and write together until brunch. We work until mid day. I will sometimes take a nap and am ready to go for the afternoon. This keeps my work at its best when I am free of any brain fog or tired. This is because I stay up later than Greg. We pretty much get up at the same time, so I need to catch up with extra rest. Sometimes we both just go sketch to get our brains working so we can be creative. For this we have a **creativity room** with many art products and tables. Our projects are always available to do something, whenever we feel like doing them. Sometimes, Greg will do some social media, audio or whatever tickles his fancy, while I am napping, gardening, painting or writing.

Then we get together to work again and stop for supper. If we do any overtime, its because we have a deadline or some extra energy. But once work is done we have what we call, **sacred time**. We have a rhythm in our schedule and when work is done for the day, we turn over our white boards and close the writing/coaching room for the day. If we have any additional work to do that requires an office, we have an office for that too. We have created an environment in our home to coincide with our lifestyle, including business.

The way that we can **maintain such connection and** congruency as a couple, so that our work and relationship flows, is we have **learned how each other learns**. More significantly, we have learned the most effective way that we learn together.

4. Seeking To Understand And How To Be Supportive - By Greg

How do two fiercely independent people, having been apart for 12 years, end up married and choose to launch a business together? We had to figure out how to **stay connected, congruent and maintain harmony** — in the business and our marriage.

Not Greg's First Business Partnership, It Is The Best

I have had many business partnerships throughout my lifetime. As I reflect on the past, in all those partnerships, I realize they were the training-ground for being able to be in this vibrant (life and business) partnership with Amee. For me, this is the first partnership where **I feel safe and have nothing to prove**. There is an unusual level of comfort, common values and understanding.

> *What follows are my observations why this partnership and business thrives the way it does.*

The Ten Reasons Our Relationship And Business Partnership Thrives

The **first reason** I feel safe and secure is because of the personal development work I have done. I am very clear who I am, my beliefs and what I want. The **second reason** is Amethyst has also done her own personal development work. The **third reason** is we have complete confidence in one another's intentions. We know that the other always has our best interests at heart.

The **fourth reason** we continue to grow, is we communicate, we talk. We make sure to discuss a topic long enough to resolve it and make an emotional connection with each other. We give each other room to express themselves — especially when either has strong feelings, reactions or emotions. There is room for each of us to express ourselves, because our core intention is to seek-first in order to understand. This intention, is the foundation of our communication.

Listening and being curious is the **fifth reason**. Instead of reacting or taking a rigid point-of-view (POV), we keep our hearts open. We begin by first seeking to understand the others POV, especially, when one of us has a different POV, feelings or a strong emotional charge. We maintain curiosity and ask questions. When we seek first to understand, it enables us to maintain a heartfelt connection. Otherwise, it is too easy to get lost in our own projections, judgements and POV. When that happens it is easy to loose track of what the other person is actually saying and feeling.

The **sixth reason** we thrive together is we acknowledge our "third wheel". There are three parties to this business. Amethyst, myself and **us** (the marriage). Yup, our third wheel is our marriage. As mentioned, we talk about everything — life and business. Remember, we each had lives before we married, and whatever we are going through is going to be influenced by our past. In our experience, our communication/dialogue provides us the opportunity to gain insight and appreciate the context of the others POV. Plus, the dialogue is a conscious tool, which brings us together in the present moment, in a powerful collaboration.

The ability to partake in those uncomfortable conversations are one of the keys that makes this work. We are **not mis-matched** as business or life partners and that is the **seventh reason** we have a solid foundation. In my other partnerships, rigid POVs and differences killed momentum. Things would get sidetracked by arguing about strategies, tactics and who was right or wrong. Then the work flow, work ethic and vision became entangled and unresolvable differences. At first, there was a natural and automatic tendency is to either dominate or shut down. This created a mismatch — a functional disconnect. This wasted a lot of time discussing and debating minutia and not working on the business. Somehow the original vision got lost in the details, disagreements or rigid positions.

Amee and I do not get lost in our conversations. We maintain connection (**reason five**) and both work at building bridges of understanding. Which can be very challenging when one of us (me most often) gets a random insight or idea. When I experience these insights or realizations, I follow my creative muse. To me, following these ideas is like oxygen which energizes and inspires me. We both are creative and have the same need for creative self expression. It makes sense that we both meet on the common ground of respecting one another's creativity and expression.

Which is the **eighth reason** we work so well together. I have been told by Amee that I tend to live in my learning curve. While I am in the learning curve I will get an insight, idea or concept. It erupts into my awareness and I feel like a man gasping for air. Often my excitement can end up hijacking the entire conversation. Sometimes, this happens because of a conversation with Amee. Her comments or observations cast a light on my own life experiences, and this helps me connect the dots. It provides me with insight and becomes a trigger for my creative muse.

> *Note: I have had to learn how to temper this enthusiasm, and not overrun Amethyst and others.*

Amethyst has the capacity to encourage me to follow my muse. This is where the knowledge that we have each other's backs (reason three) comes into play. I also need to allow room for Amee to follow her need for creative expression too.

The opportunity and challenge is to figure out how to make room for the other to follow their muse, and do it in a way that does not squish their creative inspiration or edit the others idea/concept. In the excitement of ideation it is easy for me to dominate a conversation. This creates creative tension, which always seeks resolution.

The **ninth reason** is our ability to step into this creative tension. This is very important and a key ingredient to what makes our partnership work.

We are in the truest sense, co-creators, collaborators and business partners. Often our creative direction is in complete alignment. Understand, there are times when it seems our creative direction differs. We have found that if we persist in being curious, we will understand the others POV, the outcome/result is always better.

It is like Amee has one piece of the puzzle and I have the other. Choosing to step into the creative tension together and exploring our differences, we come together. Our combined perspective completes the picture.

I have to admit that I can tend to be distracted. Fortunately, Amee knows when to speak up to get my attention and get me refocused. Sometimes we allow ourselves to follow one another's creative muse. Otherwise we might end up ignoring an important insight or catalyst for change. Which leads us to the final point, functional compromise.

The **tenth reason** our business and relationship thrives is we always seem to be able to find a functional compromise when our views differ. This is partly because we have the ability to remain curious when differences arise. Because we know, we have each other's best interests at heart (reason three).

Compromise is never a four letter word. As long as we maintain our connection, seek to understand and stay curious, we grow. When conflict or differences arise we keep talking. We will change up where we work, go to a whiteboard or take a break. We respect and encourage one another to maintain the creative urge and flow. We do not allow ourselves to become mismatched. We keep our third business partner — our relationship, the marriage, in mind.

Because "how" we do something doesn't really matter, as long as we end up at the agreed upon destination, intact, excited and fully present.

5. Our Observations About Loving Life & Learning Together

This topic, growing and working together as a couple/partners, is near and dear to us. The previous chapters were all about our personal perspectives. What we would like to share now is our observations (as a couple who are also business partners) about what we have learned about life, business and relationships.

Increased Sensitivity (A Challenge and an Opportunity)

We have observed that couples who are also business partners, have some of the greatest challenges at work and at home. When one area suffers, so does the other. There isn't a person on the planet that can completely **compartmentalize** life and separate their business from their life.

We have learned that what you do in your life and business has to be in **alignment**. When there is something incongruent, it affects everything else. As married business partners, there is greater sensitivity to one another. When someone is having an off day it affects the other and the business too. In addition, when one is having a great day, it lifts the other and when we are both having a great day, it is an amazing experience.

There Is No Business Without Life

What happens between your ears (thoughts), affects how you think of yourself, others and the business. You can have the perfect plan, but if your thoughts are negative or toxic — you will struggle to execute your plan.

The most important thing you can do is to **clean up your internal environment** and maintain alignment with your intentions.

> *Your ability to deliver a quality experience in business or in relationships with others in your life is determined by what goes on between your ears.*

When there is stinking thinking, it leads to low quality decisions. All your excitement, aspirations and hopes for your business will struggle to rise above your **internal noise or self talk**. Your self talk either becomes a roadblock or the fuel of inspiration which fires your imagination. The good news is you have 100% control over what you think about.

Is There Work Life Equilibrium?

Nobody, including you - can escape how the past has shaped you. It is **impossible to separate your business from your life**; you are who you are in both circumstances. Every conversation, success or challenge influences what you do and shapes your identity.

Even if you think you can keep your personal life separate from work, you can't. Why?

> *You are still **shaped** by the things you experience at work and at home.*

Obviously, the work/home dynamic can have a significant influence on the way a couple feels, which impacts how they respond and make business decisions.

Finding our equilibrium is a very personal thing. We can have differences in how we unwind, cope and communicate under pressure. In our experience, what's important is to make sure we are **practicing self care**. When we practice self care, equilibrium seems to take care of itself.

Comfort Zone versus Growth Zone

When you embark on launching a business together, as a couple, you are in a sense embracing a second act in your life. Everything you try now, as a couple in business, is going to be different and new. What you tried before is not necessarily relevant.

What was comfortable and relevant takes on a whole new life when you have a partner. **Working together makes everything new.**

Everything you need to become as a couple and business partners, typically lies **outside the comfort zone**. It is called the growth zone. You must stay connected to stay in sync so that one does not feel left behind or irrelevant.

Each Of You Brings A Gift To The Partnership

The gift you bring to your partnership and every relationship is **your silent, active witness**. Your active witness lies in the corridor between your conscious and subconscious awareness.
Throughout your life, this silent, active witness has been with you. It knows when you have been living a lie or are incongruent with your identity. We are not talking about all the negativity you tell yourself. We are talking about the naked, raw, undeniable truth of your existence. It exists on its own plane. Separate from the stories, drama, pain or negativity you sell yourself to others, everyone does.

We like to think of it as the silent witness which has been impartially recording every single thought, experience and word ever spoken to you. You will hear us refer to it as The Lost Guru™. You can learn to find your Lost Guru and begin to access the wisdom of your entire life experience. This is a **profound opportunity to awaken** from your socialized, programmed sleep and begin to learn from your own personal "genie in a bottle". It is a rock solid teacher, guide and friend you will learn to trust.

Couples Decision Making

When couples in business are in reaction mode they make bad decisions which affect the company. So you can end up in perpetual crisis, debt or even bankruptcy.

If you are not in harmony with your vision and the results you want in life and business, as a couple or as individuals, you end up chasing after the wrong things, at the wrong time for the wrong reasons. Couples and businesses implode when the connection disappears, love wanes and commitment vanishes.

> *So **connection and communication is key**. Its all about talking things though and being transparent about your feelings, thoughts, aspirations and dreams.*

Loving life and learning together is "the" strategy to keeping the connection alive and well; loving life and learning together is the tie that binds your hearts and your business together.

There is nothing of greater importance.

6. About Amee Dickson

Amee's Sonnet of Declaration

I am a kind, caring and gentle woman. I declare that I have time for kind, caring and intentional souls in my life.

I see the potential in every unique personality. I choose to look beyond appearances to see what might be. To see what they could become. I support honest, kind and generous souls who truly desire to grow. I am an instrument of peace and embrace all who are seeking peace.

I am an intentional woman who finds the equilibrium between strength of character and compassion in action. I have a diverse and dynamic empathic quality and use that gift in my interactions within and with other people. I am on a personal path to mastery to explore my potential in practical, balanced and gentle ways. I am a free spirit seeking to expand my entire life experience. I love variety, diversity and creativity.

My life is an extension of the creative energy of the All That Is. I am a channel for good, loving and peaceful expressions. I am open to everything that is loving, peaceful and life giving. Life is the progressive realization of living in the now and accepting "what is" in the present moment. I embrace the dance that is called life.

I Am An Esoteric Existentialist

I believe that I am solely responsible for giving meaning and significance to my life. And it is my sole responsibility and opportunity to live it with passion, sincerity and authenticity. I have been fortunate, to find someone with whom I can share "loving life and learning together".

> *I am an existentialist. I believe in the philosophical studies, that I am a human and am not merely a thinking-object, but an acting, feeling, living human person.* ***My predominant value is freedom and my primary virtue is authenticity.*** *To be authentic and real, is the only way to make sense of what I may perceive to be chaotic, meaningless, and absurd in the world, as I see it at times. Being that I am a human being that has feelings, I self-express through my actions. Thats what it means to be human. And in my opinion, love to me is a verb.*

For me, the only **meaning that there is to life is the experience of it**. My best path forward is to experience it in the present, which is the only real point of power, and the apex of change.
I am endeavouring to understand life through the lens of the human experience. We are each standing at a moment in time where we get to choose our experience.

Up until now, Amee has been in training.

My life seemed to be made up of 10 year increments of what I call life stages, composed of a multitude of very crucial moments for me. Through the learning experiences of my life, I have been able to tap into the lessons, of those defining moments, that I graduated through. I have learned who I am, who I am not, what I want less of, and what I want more of. So its been an inner journey.

I can now see how each piece of the puzzle brought me one step closer to a greater understanding of myself. I learned how to make the decisions to honour my wellbeing. I can now use those skills to address challenges today as they arise. I hone those skills from my past and use them as magic wands to create rainbows of adventure and intrigue.

All of those phases were each significant in their own way. However, that which I feel was the greatest phase was in the last decade. It was the most tumultuous time period because it provided the most information I would need to sum up and connect the dots. I entered into a new life of self-awareness, understanding and awakening.

Artist, Author, Serial Entrepreneur and Coach

Like many professional women, I worked, raised a family, maintained the family home and went to University. What makes my path unique, is along the way, I built three businesses while pursuing my professional and educational interests. As a mature, conscious and intentional woman, what fascinates me lies at the intersection of science, psychology and personal development.

When people ask about my background, I share my experience coaching women and families in crisis, my extensive involvement as a volunteer and 10 years of post secondary education.

I consider it a sincere honour to support, Coach and mentor other like minded individuals. I welcome the opportunity to meet or speak with you and learn about your journey.

Amee's Principle: The Power to Choose

The principle of the power to choose is always active, available and awaiting my command. I always have the opportunity to choose to engage with this principle, that enhances my life, at any given moment. With this power to choose, I live a life that is meaningful and brings significance and joy according to **my own beliefs, values, morals and ethics**. This principle allows me to live a life of freedom and autonomy, which is sacred to me. Living incongruent with my beliefs robs me of everything I uphold to be true and dear to me.

Amee's Principle: Self-Respect And Living With Dignity

When I respect myself, I teach others how to treat me. I value self honesty. Part of living with dignity involves staying honest. Therefore, self-accountability and self-responsibility are my mottos. I am true to my integrity and I don't stomp on my birthrights to love, joy, peace, safety and security, and well-being. I feel worthy of happiness and I am comfortable using my voice. I am, without apology, and the need to be right.

Amee's Principle: Integrity

Integrity means my personal congruence, otherwise I lose face in my own eyes and I respect myself less. That means I say what I mean and mean what I say. I trust people who keep their word. So if I commit to something, I have to be willing and ready to follow through. I'd like to think I am fair. I make every attempt to demonstrate honesty and integrity, by living it. I also feel I must be consistent. I make an effort to be authentic and genuine.

The gist of my self-integrity is all about making peace within myself, and that I am living congruent with my morals, ethics, values, principles, faith, and beliefs. My behaviour must reflect that, if I am to be fully engaging in the laws of integrity.

7. About Greg Dickson

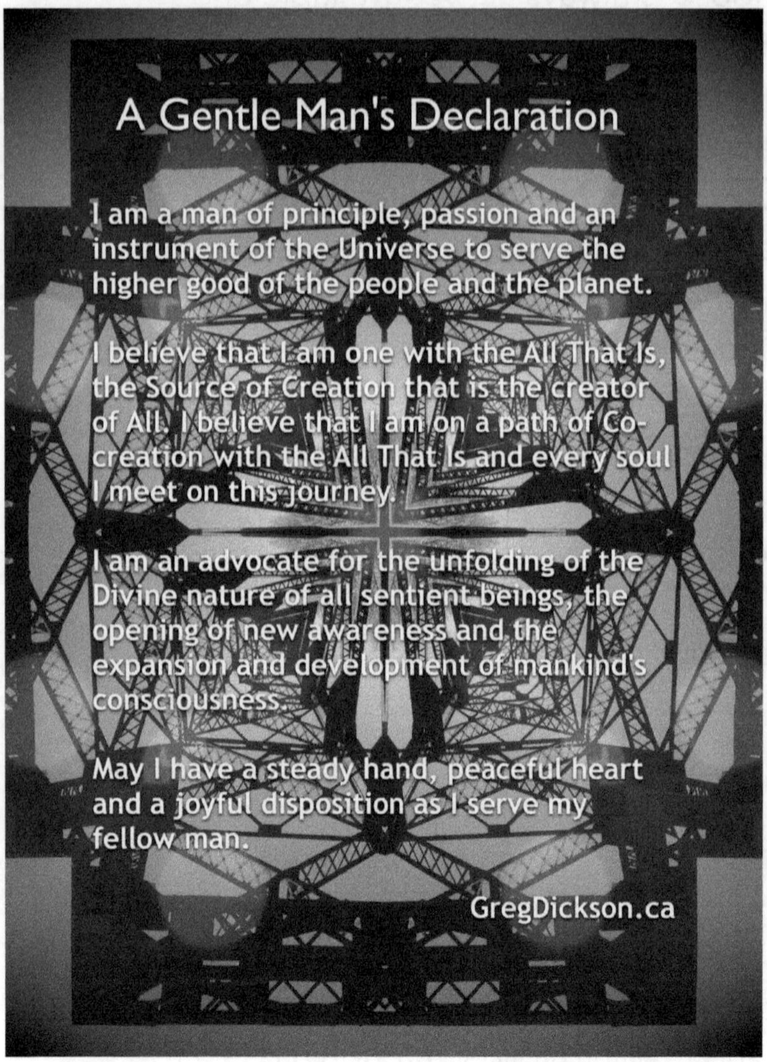

A Gentleman's Declaration

My life has never been the same since the day I wrote this declaration. It was an awakening that unfolded as I sought answers from the All That Is, following a painful life experience.

I am a man of principle, passion and an instrument of the Universe to serve the higher good of the people and the planet.

I believe that I am one with the All That is, the Source of Creation that is the creator of All. I believe that I am on a path of Co-creation with the All That Is and every soul I meet on this journey.

I am an advocate for the unfolding of the Divine nature of all sentient beings, the opening of a new awareness and the expansion and development of mankind's consciousness. May I have a steady hand, peaceful heart and a joyful disposition as I serve my fellowman.

Author, Coach, Entrepreneur

Over the years I was able to build an disability insurance practice, a printing brokerage, an entrepreneurial training company, a creative design agency, business coaching practice, a web development business and wrote two business books. I stopped counting the number of people I've coached and trained (10,000+) and what I'm most proud is that I've had the honour of coaching and supporting business owners and entrepreneurs in more than 35 industries.

Living & Working With Integrity

My life long passion has been in the pursuit of living and working with integrity. From my early days as a young entrepreneur delivering a quality product and service was always my top priority. As a coach and consultant, guiding and supporting my clients to figure out their own way to live and work with integrity, has been rewarding and challenging. In a noisy world that is clamouring for our attention and our trust, maintaining ones integrity is paramount.

My work for decades, as a business coach, has given me a unique perspective to the integrity question. Every single consumer expects us to treat them with respect and integrity. The great challenge for entrepreneurs, is staying true to ones own values, beliefs, morals and ethics while conducting business successfully — without destroying other people's values, beliefs, morals and ethics. When this happens you become the living embodiment of your integrity. This is our greatest challenge and a significant opportunity.

My joy and personal pleasure is to serve and guide clients on their own unique journey to live and work with integrity. It is with this mission and focus that Life Origami Corporation was formed with my wife Amethyst Dickson.

Whether or not you are an entrepreneur, the challenge and the opportunity is the same, to understand ones own values, beliefs, morals and ethics — then figure out how to live and work accordingly. It is the most important foundation upon which you can build a successful life or business.

I am proud of the work that Amethyst and I have done, to bring Life Origami forward to serve people like you. It is with great respect and care that we conduct business, share our ideas and support our clients. All of this is with an eye on living and working with integrity, in alignment with our values, beliefs, morals and ethics. This is the Life Origami way.

8. It's Not the Critic Who Counts

"It is not the critic who counts; not the man who points out how the strong man stumbles, or where the doer of deeds could have done them better. The credit belongs to the man who is actually in the arena, whose face is marred by dust and sweat and blood; who strives valiantly; who errs, who comes short again and again, because there is no effort without error and shortcoming; but who does actually strive to do the deeds; who knows great enthusiasms, the great devotions; who spends himself in a worthy cause; who at the best knows in the end the triumph of high achievement, and who at the worst, if he fails, at least fails while daring greatly, so that his place shall never be with those cold and timid souls who neither know victory nor defeat." — Theodore Roosevelt, Citizen in a Republic , (speech), 1910

9. How This Book Evolved

What you are reading began as a result of a conversation Amethyst and I had in November 2017. We started a few writing projects before this one and this version went through five iterations.

When we began writing our intention was to bring forward a book titled "Enough! A Love Story" which was about falling in love again, with yourself. We realized that when we came together as a couple, it was only because we had reconnected with our true essence. This resulted in a new level of self love and acceptance.

On the long road to creating this book, Amethyst and I came to a realization — that without the foundation of self love and self acceptance — we might never have reconnected. Why? Had we not broken through the cocoon in which we had taken refuge — our old Caterpillar selves would still be crawling through life. This would have been a real shame.

It was a shared epiphany. We realized that the foundation of all relationships is built upon the foundation of the relationship we have with ourselves. We believe that in the daily process of our expanding self acceptance, we have an opportunity. We have a choice — no, an obligation to do whatever we can — to fully inhabit our lives. Like the Butterfly, we took the time in cocoon to heal, transform and love ourselves.

The Epiphany of The Lost Guru™ Uncovered

Amee recounts... In 2017, before I reunited with Greg, I had been studying a series of recordings about unleashing the power of the female brain by Dr. Amen. I was very much interested in the subject of how the brain worked. I had been studying the role of emotions and the brain. I had been writing notes for many years on various topics about self-improvement and I attended many conventions dedicated to this.

In fact I read a book by a famous self-help guru and he was promising to teach all these invaluable guidelines to improve a persons lot in life. I scoured the book seeking to locate the "guidelines" and could not find the actual sections he alluded to. I was very disappointed because I was hoping to find the answers to my puzzles in life, but all I could find was the rah rah pep rally's.

As I reflected upon all the research and reading I did, it felt like none of the circumstances were pertinent to me. The solutions described by these authors didn't seem to fit me.

So about that same time, Greg and I met up, we spent a lot of time talking about what I had been learning and writing about. We discussed the self-help industry at length. At the time, Greg was writing a book called Headstrong and Heartfelt, Beyond the Pain. Living With Your Shadow. The shadow he alluded to was grief.

So we remarked about how our interests had changed in the years since we found each other. We talked about our pasts and discovered we had similar stories about being down in the trenches, and then arising like a lotus flower in murky waters.

When we thought about what had caused us to be in the situations we found ourselves in over the last decade, we surmised that the common trait we both suffered from was the thought virus of "I am not enough, I am broken, I need to be fixed." In fact, I wrote a journal of 132 pages on that topic, as to why I stayed stuck in that state and how I got there.
I read it to Greg and it was very much like the book he was writing. Yet, somehow, someway we had been changing and evolving. As we confided

in each other, we were both healing. The clouds of confusion lifted along with our spirits. In fact, many people called us "excessively happy".

We thought about how we came together. We shared how much work we had to do to get to the point where we would open up, give ourselves permission to let someone into our lives. We were surprised to learn that we each, around similar timeframes, had given ourselves permission to dream and live the dream again. And we discovered that the necessary component of being able to do this was, we had to learn that we were enough, and more, so much more.

At the time, Greg and I had been keeping a joint journal. We had been writing quite a bit about the experience of being loved, loving each other as well as ourselves. We wanted to share the idea of our gratitude book with others. Quickly, that idea morphed into writing a book called "Enough! A love story." We worked on it and had quite a few chapters similar to what our program "Mastering the Art of Momentum" contains.

And so we talked about these philosophical ideas constantly. In the spring of 2018, Greg and I went to the Indianapolis 500. It was a 13 day trip there and back by car. When we weren't touring and sleeping or eating, we were driving (and taking pictures of the scenery). We travelled about 8000 km and we went through 11 states and provinces in the USA and Canada. It was a long ride in a short amount of time. So we spent a long time in the car talking about our book, business and what we were learning.

I told Greg how I read a book recently about how to live a life unbound, but it didn't actually tell a person how to do it. Then Greg had an epiphany.

Greg observes ... We became excited to finally understand what the key component of the self-help industry was, which always seemed to be missing.

Self-help gurus were providing the philosophies and psychology of change, but what was missing were the skills and tools to allow people to actually integrate it into their lives. And what seemed to work for one guru and his other amazing followers, was useless information to another.

We discovered the missing link. What was missing was that every person is different. We all learn differently, have different beliefs, values, morals and ethics than others. And most important — we each have a different context — of life experiences. This context, as it turns out is everything. The context of your life experience also contains the lessons, insights and wisdom you need to fully inhabit your life.

We started to see that if people could just tap into their own life experiences and extract the lessons from those experiences, their lives would change rapidly. We believed that they actually could learn enough about themselves, from themselves, to teach themselves about who they are and what they want in life. They would just need to learn to get into touch with this "Inner Guru" and learn how to access its wisdom.

We believed that if they could learn how to tap into their inherent wisdom, from their past, they would be able to toggle through life's challenges. In fact, they would no longer settle for survival, they would need to learn how to weave their way through this learning maze to come out ahead in the end.

See, we believe that there was an inner wisdom that builds and grows throughout your lifetime. Not only that, every single soul has a treasure house of untapped potential. Once you realize it is there and learn how to access and work with it, you would now be accelerating and learning about oneself according to "You-how" rather than "Others-how". What works for one person may be useless to another. Face it, not everybody can live their life like these gurus, because they are not those people nor do they have the context of their experiences, nor the skills they've acquired. Just like nobody else does me as good as me. Nobody can be me. Nobody else can be you.

Upon learning this, we examined how our skills and tools came about as a result of the lessons we had extracted throughout our lives, and how it helped us to come out ahead.

We decided that it would be more helpful to others by teaching them how we learned to graduate through defining moments, and get on living.

> *We wanted to share our tools and skills so that others could learn from themselves. It would be far more useful for people to learn from themselves and be able to take on any challenge with confidence in the future.*

So in the beginning, we focused on writing articles and recording podcasts. That evolved into a website as a place to make our articles available, in addition to social media.

Amee reflects ... Slowly, day by day since 2018, we have continued to explore, test and perfect our approach. We came up with a program incorporating everything I had used in my past, and Greg had used in his life, to grow and change. We incorporated all the tools, tactics and strategies that we used to help ourselves and others — in crisis or making major changes in their lives — into our program. As well, we had been writing some pretty cool stuff about how to get on with life and get past all the roadblocks.

Greg had a vast amount of experience in teaching and coaching over the 30 years plus. We felt that we needed to explain to people how to accelerate through the learning curve to get on with life, and to learn how to thrive rather than simply survive. These articles that we were writing, all came together to discuss this very topic in this book.

We also wanted to share what we had been learning about couples and partners in life and business. We were having so many profound experiences, we just had to share this with other like minded couples or anyone partnering with another in life or business.

In the past, we knew what it was like to have relationships and business partners pull us down and stop us from successfully finding joy in our lives. So we began to write about communication and connections as couples and life/business partners. And that's how the book began to take shape.

Our purpose in writing this book is to introduce you to the concept that you are The Lost Guru™. Our secondary purpose is to introduce you to the key issues and core concepts, you will need to embrace, if you are going to live an intentional and conscious reality.

A few years ago Greg had a profound insight, "You cannot experience what you will not confront, examine, release and embrace." This book was written with the intent to help you confront and examine what has been holding you back from fully inhabiting your life.

We intentionally did not address the release and embrace modalities in this book because it is not possible to create movement on these major life and consciousness issues without in person support, training and coaching.

> NOTE: our program, Mastering The Art of Momentum takes participants through the entire transformation experience which includes confront, examine, release and embrace.

Four Core Messages of This Book

You will observe four core messages woven throughout this book:

1. The **Guru** you seek is **already** within you.

2. You don't know what you want, even though you think you do. This is because you haven't spent the time to figure it out. You stop yourself because you feel you aren't enough. You feel you aren't worthy of more, so you don't indulge the idea. You don't trust yourself with the dream in the first place.
3. We all commit the Ultimate Crime, we deny our weaknesses and our greatness. We do this because we are not confronting and examining the roadblocks to our success.
4. Growing and learning together is the most important factor to help you navigate the path of communication and connection in relationships. It will keep you on track pointed toward fully inhabiting your life.

We are going to stop here and resist the urge to explain and summarize this entire book. The trick is to read it, contemplate it and see if there is a part of you that awakens while reading it. Take a look and see what you might learn and discover about yourself.

One thing we know for sure. You do not have to live any longer with self doubt, anxiety, confusion, frustration or self loathing. Your secrets are within you, and your Lost Guru™ will give you the keys to open your mind and your heart.

So if you are ready to dive into some self honesty, gain some fresh insights and explore how you can recover from the crime of self denial, then welcome. We look forward to your feedback and questions. You can find our contact info at the back of this book.

Are You Ready To Take The Next Step To Fully Inhabit Your Life?

If you're still reading/listening we think you are ready to get on with getting real. Therefore, if you are going to escape the toxic hamster wheel of unconscious existence then it is time to make a shift away from denial, avoidance and busyness and begin to confront reality — the way things are.

If you want to ever "fully inhabit" your life, you will have to step away from the mundane, toxic, lazy, habitual thinking patterns. You will have to learn how to stop indulging in ceaseless projection, blame, judgement and obsessive overthinking.

> *If there are parts of this book that have resonated with you or you felt like you learned something, we would love to hear about it from you. It will encourage us and help us understand whether you want to hear more like this from us.*

At Life Origami, our goal is to educate you how you can take proactive action, so you do not end up having to panic and call the fire department because your life is on fire. You have the ability to rescue yourself and escape the jaws of uncertainty, doubt and fear.

> *We educate our clients in methods they can use to* ***take back control of their lives and fully embrace their Individuality****. Move from a grey, boring existence to one of passion, confidence and clarity.*

We do that through our signature teaching on the **Four Laws of Individuality**. We believe there are four laws, like gravity, that are acting silently upon our individuality. They are as such: **Self Care, Self-Expression, Mastery and Progress**. These four laws directly, quietly and consistently act upon our lives. Our awareness is peaked as we grow and evolve.

As we begin to assert our individuality, explore our uniqueness and need for originality, to form our identity and character - we naturally begin to embrace and celebrate our need for “separateness”.

To the degree that we are able to embrace this "separateness" and explore what it means to truly be ourselves, develop character and a clear identity — we begin to switch from surviving to thriving. To learn about how our 4 week and long term (15 to 18 month) training enhanced coaching programs unfold, keep reading.

Discover Your Lost Guru: Coaching Package

Are Ready To Uncover The Mental Habits That Prevent You From Tapping Into The Wisdom Of Your Life?

> If so, you and are just one decision away from embarking on a unique, life defining adventure.

This is the four (4) week course companion to The Lost Guru Ebook. It includes 3 X 1 hour coaching sessions and a 2 hour Emotional Release session.

4 Week Training Enhanced Coaching Opportunity

What You Will Learn

- How to identify your dream killers, know the patterns, habits and mindsets which drain your energy.
- Learn that you have a hidden treasure of wisdom that you can tap into from your own life.
- Know that at any time, you have the power of choice to access the support and insights of your Active Witness (a.k.a. Lost Guru).

- Understand what has been blocking you from tapping into your Lost Guru.
- You will learn what stops you and/or how you take yourself out of the game.
- You will understand the components that make for a healthy drive."
- Know the elements which contribute to experiencing flow and congruent self connection.
- Have a basic understanding of what it takes to retrain your brain to serve and not hinder you.
- Learn how it is possible to influence your mind to serve your highest and best interests. Instead, you will stop being enslaved to subconscious habitual habits.

4 Week Program Outline

Week 1: Read chapter 1 of The Lost Guru Book, watch "what you need to know about The Lost Guru" video, followed by your 1st coaching session with Amethyst and Greg Dickson to help you "Tap into the Inherent Wisdom" of your life (1 hour).

Week 2: Read chapter 2 of The Lost Guru book, watch Habits, Patterns & Obstacles video, 2nd coaching session to identify the "Habits, Patterns & Obstacles" preventing you from experiencing your greatness (1 hour).

Week 3: Experience the Life Origami, Emotional Release Technique, guided meditation and emotional release session. The Emotional release technique is a guided imagery process that supports you to fully release the old patterns, habits, and stories you may be clinging to. It is a process that will clear the decks of past traumas, pain and anxiety once and for all. You will be surprised how you feel afterward and how effortless it is for you to move forward in life. (2 hours)

Week 4: Your final coaching call is a Q&A session to help you integrate what you have learned. The goal of this session is to help you identify the roadblocks and obstacles you discovered in your previous sessions and self study. We will support you to prioritize your next steps and discuss how you can begin to build a relationship with your Lost Guru.

What You Get

This four (4) week Training Enhanced Coaching program is just $500 and includes:

- 3 one hour, 2-on-1 coaching calls with Greg and Amethyst
- The 2 hour Life Origami Emotional Release Session
- Video and Audio Trainings
- Self Assessment Questionnaire
- The Lost Guru ebook: This book will help you to uncover the mental habits that prevent you from tapping into the wisdom of your life.
- Q&A email access to Greg and Amethyst

The past is gone, your only point of power is now…

> Consider this, how would the quality of your life change if you knew you had the support, mentoring, training and tools to help you to Fully Inhabit Your Life? You owe it to yourself to learn more…

Take your first step — Call Greg or Amee at 1-403-307-8281.

About Our 18 Month Training Enhanced Coaching Program

Mastering The Art of Momentum

Mastering the Art of Momentum is the complete training enhanced coaching series which integrates 16 Life Origami training modules. Each module progressively builds through four phases:

Phase 1. Living With Ease
Phase 2. Mindset Matters
Phase 3. Insights, Identity and Individuality, and concludes with
Phase 4. Building Bridges of Understanding

What makes this program unique is the combination of online, self paced learning and 2-on-1 coaching sessions over the course of 15 to 18 months. Each designed to get you into a place of consistency and congruent actions, to ensure you experience what you want. Because each person has a different pace and style of learning and growing, the program's length is variable. This ensures you have the time needed to fully integrate what you have learned about yourself and your magnificent obsession.

Our program utilizes a two week rotation of self-study followed by a 2-on-1 coaching session. This pattern, one week self study followed by a week of follow up coaching is designed to assist you to accelerate your learning and actually integrate transformational change.

In week one, teaching and training videos provide you with the foundational principles and insights to understand the key issues and opportunities for long-term change. This is followed by self study, reflective exercises and homework designed to empower you to identify, observe and explore your own insights, issues and personal lessons.

The following week, your 2-on-1 coaching session begins. Amee and Greg support you to integrate what you've learned in the training to overcome inertia, work through any obstacles and achieve your most meaningful and significant experiences. This approach ensures you have the mindset, skills, tools, training and coaching to create the desired results and movement in your life and business — what we call momentum.

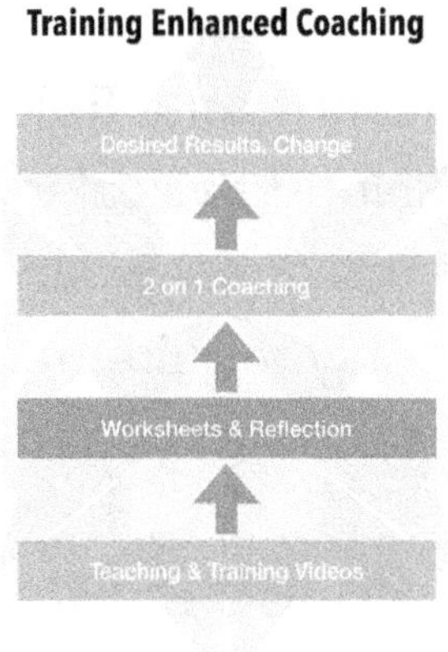

Procrastination disappears, fear is contained and you begin to feel stronger and more confident. You will find yourself doing the right things, at the right time for the right reasons. Your energy and identity soars as you shed the shackles of the past. You begin to witness yourself consistently manifesting your highest ideals and desired results. Clarity builds as you begin to focus on the sub purposes within the action plan you'll create for living your dream.

Phase 1: Living With Ease

This is a distinct set of processes and experiences which will take you to new levels of awareness and an opportunity to connect with a clearer vibrational state. People report experiencing the release of physical, emotional, and psychological trauma. This will create

a clean internal and external environment which will become a foundation for you to build upon.

The Four Laws Intake Assessment: This assessment sets a foundation for your Life Origami journey. This is a facilitated self assessment process designed to provide you with a holistic point of view of your current life, situation including gaps in mindset, skills, training and coaching priorities.

Emotional First Aid: You will learn a powerful breathing and visualization technique that you can use to reset your focus, calm your mind and heart, anywhere, anytime.

Emotional Release Technique: This is a metaphysical Energy Release of Non-Physical, negative and/or toxic emotional energy. The story behind the energy, why it happened, and who is to blame is not important. The only requirement for ERT to work is that you are ready to release, and truly let go of your attachment to your story around your issue(s).

Phase 2: Mindset Matters

Your life becomes manifest based upon your internal dialogue. A positive or negative mindset tends to be a generator of a self fulfilling prophecy. It is your internal compass that directs your attention, energy and impacts the quality of your life.

Mindset Matters

Thought Audit: This is all about having a healthy self talk environment. Everything begins in the mind including our projections, judgments and perceptions of who we are, what we deserve and who we choose to share our life with. This all begins with a healthy mind. As a result of this process, you will become aware of areas of your life and thoughts that may be producing net negative or net positive impacts. This will make it easier to make decisions to move forward. You will be able to quickly assess whether the people, situations, and your thoughts are producing a net negative or net positive effect on your life.

You will no longer feel held captive by toxic, traumatic, or disturbing thoughts that drag you down. When exploring the potential for net positive effects in your life, you will let go of the negative weight that came from your attachments and self judgments. You will make a shift towards exploring more possibilities for your life experiences.

Your Identity Story (Frame-of-Reference): Everyone assimilates a personal frame of reference. As we travel through life we acquire other people's opinions, beliefs and perspectives. Some of them we consciously choose, but most are simply adopted and unexamined. In this process you will know your frame of reference and be able to recreate it at will.

Brain Mastery: You will learn techniques to leverage the neuroplastic power of your brain. Together we will design a set of activities and experiences which will rewire your brain, so you can intentionally connect with your world and then choose how to respond, instead of reacting unconsciously.

Phase 3: Insights, Identity & Individuality

You will embrace and explore who you are as an individual with your own way of thinking, distinct personality. The process of acknowledging the inherent wisdom of your life creates a confident, solid foundation. This is the prime purpose of this phase, to build one's life and/or business upon the unique wisdom of your active witness.

Insights, Individuality and Identity

Lost Guru: Overcome the fear of being alone, and feeling lost and confused in life. You can do this by learning how to tap into the wisdom of your "active witness", that has been accumulating over your lifetime. This is a live teaching, intuition & insight session to introduce you to your active witness (aka lost guru) and ask questions. The session will be recorded so that you can listen to it at your leisure. It is a message of compassion, insight, encouragement and love. Time frame is one 1.5 hour session each. They cannot be done back to back, it depends on the flow. After this occurs you will need quiet time to journal and self care. At the conclusion, participants will feel a greater sense of connection with their own inner guru (life force).

Life Force Anchoring: This unique experience is a hybrid of Reiki with a channeled message session which will introduce you to your active witness.

F.U.N.- This is a facilitated dialogue to explore and expand the understanding of your Lost Guru and how FUN has been an active witness to your F.U.N. factor over your lifetime. This will shine a light on your life purpose which is your journey of self-discovery and personal expression.

Transformation Sequence: The TS is a reflective process you can use to coach yourself through the thinking and emotional obstacles that keep you stuck, and prevent forward movement. You will learn how to design your own tangible path forward - so you can fully inhabit your life. You are going to experience the four phases of transformation which are practical, applicable, scientific and leads to personal congruency.

Life Compass: When you feel confused and need to make decisions or adjustments when unexpected circumstances occur, you will be able to use your customized life compass. It will help you get back on track and in alignment with your highest values. You will be able to gain sudden clarity and direction for your life anywhere, anytime. The process is a 1.5 hour to 2 hour facilitated session (for each person) that results in 1 (each) mind map. This is used to create a custom life compass wallpaper for your smart phone.

Phase 4: Building Bridges of Understanding™

You will take all your new insights and understandings, including your new mindset and intentions, and get into action. You will begin putting your attention upon your intentions, using your new identity and create movement, which manifests your highest ideals and desired results. You will focus on the sub purposes within an action plan to begin living your dream.

The Natural Art of Self Promotion: If you are going to Fully Inhabit Your Life, you will need other peoples help, support, cooperation and collaboration. You have natural self promotion tendencies. In this section of your training and coaching we help you put your "support and cooperation story" together in a congruent and coherent fashion.

Psychological Anchors: There are some general patterns of human behaviour and tendencies. In this section, we provide you with insights, perspectives about how to approach different types of people. This way, you will be able to align with people whop have different dispositions, viewpoints and values.

Conversational Leadership (COINS): This communication training series will enhance and expand your abilities to make heartfelt connections with the people in your life. It will help you build community, while providing the leadership to help others solve problems, make decisions and improve the quality of their lives. You will learn the COINS pneumonic which is a conversational framework to ask open ended questions, and expand your listening skills. Not only will you be able to influence people, but you will also have the tools and structure to resolve conflicts and come to a harmonious agreement in any life situation.

Learning Curve Acceleration: This is the science of human drive and advanced problem solving. You will be able to learn your way out of any situation, puzzle or dilemma. You are going to learn how to truly leverage your curiosity, gain insights and accelerate your growth. You will be able to shift into being an observer and find balance between your willingness to learn and willingness to change. You will gain personal insights to empower you to make decisions, alter your course and confront reality when things don't turn out the way you want.

Dream Bridge™: This training builds upon all of the skills, shifts and momentum that you have achieved and learned throughout your journey in the program. It is an accelerated planning technique which eliminates the tyranny of traditional goal setting, planning, productivity and performance philosophies. You will acquire a little known secret that will allow you to create results without all the roadblocks, tensions, fear and anxiety. It will change the way you view planning forever. It's a 7 step framework that ends with a concrete actionable plan.

Life Navigation Wheel™: We pull information from your answers to the 4 Laws Self Assessment and your action plan from your Dream Bridge. As well, we include the insights you gained while travelling your training enhanced coaching program, in order to create your unique Life Navigation Wheel. It will provide you with direction in four areas; self care, self expression, mastery and progress. You will understand your current opportunities to make life more meaningful and significant. You will know what you can do to ensure you feel a sense of security and wellbeing. In addition, you will gain a sense of control over your life and clarity about what it will take to achieve your dreams and goals. You will learn how to tap into the intrinsic urge to bend, fold and shape life to your will, whims, and wishes. Clarity will rise to help you convert your undeveloped strengths into competencies. You will receive training on the 4 laws of individuality and the 8 ways to actively engage with the laws.

Living Your Dream Celebration: From your "Dream Bridge" learning journey you will be given the opportunity to create your very own "Living The Dream" action plan and use it as a learning example and actually begin living your dream.

If you feel like you have more potential to experience something more, you owe it to yourself to follow through to explore what might be possible for you. Our humble goal is to awaken you to your inherent potential.

Then, if you so choose, you can launch into your own journey to Fully Inhabit Your Life.

Life Origami is a co-creation of Amethyst and Greg Dickson

I (Amee) was a former coaching client of Gregs in 2006/07. In the years hence, life happened and we both ended up divorced. We closed our businesses and faced a number of lumps and bumps along life's road. In 2017, we reunited, quickly fell in love and got married. As Greg and I look back we found that **if it wasn't for our journeys, we wouldn't be together today**. We wouldn't be in such unity, harmony and experiencing the greatest love of our lives. We lived different lives and each had to learn to overcome adversities. We each made a **conscious choice** to extract the lessons from our life experiences. This now enables us to create a compelling life together. As a result, this has also provided a foundation to build upon and create a business too.

> *We began collaborating, sharing our journey and the lessons we extracted from the experiences over the decade we were apart. We each discovered that we had* ***developed new skills and tools*** *that we used to overcome roadblocks and challenges, and create forward movement towards a compelling life.*

Greg had actually taught me a few of these principles and a way to navigate through any circumstance or challenge in life or business. But over the 10 years that we lived separate lives, I discovered that these same principles and techniques, to be conscious, could be used in my personal life too. And I tweaked them and I was able to accelerate through challenges and opportunities as they came along. I was able to navigate and make decisions that were to the benefit of my greater good.

And Greg did the same. He learned far more over the 10 years we were apart than what he had taught me previously. So when we came together again in a relationship, we exchanged what we learned on our journeys, and we could see vast similarities. We also saw the benefits from the differences in how we each went about consciously applying them to our life and business. We quickly realized we were onto something significant. We understood that a new opportunity was unfolding. We embraced creating a complete personal and professional development experience to share with others.

With this awareness we realized that our life and businesses could not thrive without achieving a **complete inner equilibrium**. Over the years we learned that a business cannot be a separated from what is going on in ones life. And so it became the perfect opportunity to create a method that is more than just principles and goals. We found the missing thumb drive to fill the gaps in learning and how to understand ourselves and resolve the uncertainty.

Understanding and using these methodologies from our past made it possible for us to create an unbound life and experience an **unshakeable inner presence**. With this mindset, we were both able to bridge our self-awareness into meaningful congruent action, which created consistent forward movement. As a result, we were **able to coach ourselves through life** utilizing the principles of what we now call Life Origami.

Unknowingly, we both had enrolled into a method that uncovered our "YOU-How". We **tapped into our inner guru**, aware that we only needed our own inner wisdom to create the life we considered to be satisfying and fulfilling. And that was the key to cruising along our paths toward living our dreams individually and collectively.

So since coming together in 2017, we have developed an **actual tool and skill kit** to assist people like you to toggle through life's challenges. This skill and tool kit revealed itself to be so flexible, powerful and complete that we knew many could benefit. We just had to give it life and offer it to others.

We are very in-tune with the fact that everybody has challenges and could make really good use of these **inherent potentials that lie within**.

That includes you!

And so we decided that we had to figure out a way to offer the tools we developed, to connect up with other human beings, regardless of their position in life or the challenges they face. This book and our program (Chapter 9) is the result of a **lifetime of learning and two years of debate, testing and refinement**. If you have a wish to lead a happy and congruent life we want to meet you! And so, we want to encourage you to consider embarking on **your own journey of self discovery**, by reading and finishing this book, Mastering the Art of Momentum.

> *If there is anything we have said in this book that resonates with you — you owe it to yourself to explore how our program (Chapter 9) could help you to* ***shape, mold and bend life to your will, whims and wishes.***

To find out more about our 13 month program, scroll to the Chapter titled "Our 13 Month Training Enhanced Coaching Program." Where you can read an introduction to the program.

Contacting Greg or Amethyst

If you'd like to explore how the Life Origami, training enhanced coaching system can help you accelerate through the learning curve of your life, send Greg (greg@lifeorigami.com) and Amee (amee@lifeorigami.com) or give us a call at 1-403-307-8281 or @lifeorigami on Twitter or Facebook. Our website www.LifeOrigami.com always has the latest updates.

www.ingramcontent.com/pod-product-compliance
Lightning Source LLC
LaVergne TN
LVHW082354200926
848481LV00012B/3556